IS IT WELL WITH YOUR SOUL?

Discovering peace in the eye of the storm

A CIP catalogue record for this book is available from the British Library.

ISBN: 978-1-7385369-7-9

Cover design and illustration by Beth Stevenson, Care for the Family.

Typeset by John Lambert, breathe.design.

Printed and bound by Xpedient Print Services.

A Christian initiative to strengthen family life, offering support to everyone.
Care for the Family is a registered charity (England and Wales: 1066905; Scotland: SC038497).
A company limited by guarantee no. 3482910.
Registered in England and Wales. Tovey House, Cleppa Park, Newport, NP10 8BA.

'And the peace of God, which transcends all understanding, will guard your hearts and your minds in Christ Jesus.'

Philippians 4:7

FOREWORD

Often when I am speaking to an audience at one of our Care for the Family events, I will acknowledge that all manner of people will be represented in the room. While some will be enjoying what feels like a mountaintop moment in their lives, others will be encountering an unexpected and unwanted valley.

Both my own experiences, and decades of pastoral ministry, have taught me that the journey of life – with all its joys, disappointments, and heartache – does not lend itself to pausing long enough to ask, 'Is it well with my soul?'

This book was written to help us do that. Within these pages are thoughts, stories and reflections to help us consider the state of our innermost being – our hopes, fears, and deepest longings.

My prayer is that one or more of these contributions will become a means of invitation to you, where you might feel God's presence and glimpse his perspective.

Above all, wherever you find yourself – mountaintop, valley, or somewhere in between – I hope this book will help you to encounter the peace of God that is in Christ Jesus, allowing you to find his rest and an anchor for your soul.

Robin Vincent, CEO, Care for the Family

INTRODUCTION

I wonder how familiar you are with the hymn *It Is Well With My Soul*? The words of this powerful song have been sung by millions upon millions of people since it was written in 1873. Its writer, Horatio Spafford, faced more tragedy and loss than most of us could ever imagine. A successful lawyer and investor, he suffered significant financial loss due to the Great Chicago Fire of 1871. Just two years later, the ship carrying his wife and four daughters, the *Ville du Havre*, sank in the Atlantic Ocean after a collision with another vessel. Only his wife Anna survived.

As Horatio Spafford travelled to meet his wife in the days that followed this horrific incident, the ship he was on passed near to where his daughters had died. In the midst of his loss, he put pen to paper and wrote these now world-famous words:

> *When peace like a river attendeth my way,*
> *When sorrows like sea billows roll;*
> *Whatever my lot, Thou hast taught me to say,*
> *It is well, it is well with my soul.*
>
> Refrain:
> *It is well with my soul,*
> *It is well, it is well with my soul.*
>
> *Though Satan should buffet, though trials should come,*
> *Let this blest assurance control,*
> *That Christ hath regarded my helpless estate,*
> *And hath shed his own blood for my soul.*
>
> *My sin – oh, the bliss of this glorious thought!*
> *My sin, not in part but the whole,*
> *Is nailed to the cross, and I bear it no more,*
> *Praise the Lord, praise the Lord, O my soul!*

For me, be it Christ, be it Christ hence to live:
If Jordan above me shall roll,
No pang shall be mine, for in death as in life
Thou wilt whisper Thy peace to my soul.

But, Lord, 'tis for Thee, for Thy coming we wait,
The sky, not the grave, is our goal;
Oh, trump of the angel! Oh, voice of the Lord!
Blessed hope, blessed rest for my soul!

Whilst this book was in development, after many years of infertility and multiple losses, our daughter was born ten weeks early. My husband Luke and I spent the first seven weeks of her life in hospital and during that traumatic and uncertain time, I found my mind regularly returning to the story of Horatio Spafford. A man born hundreds of years before me, who lost more than most of us could even imagine, but whose faith carried him through the worst times of his life. Over 150 years later, his hymn continues to inspire people across the globe, reminding us to find peace and hope amidst life's challenges. And it was to carry Horatio and his wife Anna through further heartbreak.

The Spaffords had three more children after the deaths of their first four daughters – Grace and Bertha, and a son also named Horatio. Sadly, little Horatio died of scarlet fever at the age of four, compounding the agony for parents who had already lost four children.

This tragedy marked an epoch for the Spaffords, leading them to hold prayer meetings in their home with likeminded believers. This group became known as 'the Overcomers'.[1] They moved to Jerusalem and set up a religious community which provided social services, education and medical care.

---

[1] Library of Congress, 'Saved Alone', *American Colony in Jerusalem*, 1870 to 2006.

This community endured beyond Horatio's death at 59 of malaria, and became a movement that provided food for the starving and refuge for orphans during World War One. Today, the Spafford Children's Center in Jerusalem, founded in 1925 by their daughter Bertha, continues this work.[2] The seeds the Spaffords had sown came to beautiful fruition.

So what does it mean for it to be well with our souls today? Can these words be lived out in a way that is authentic and true? And what would a life where things are well with our souls look like in reality? And, I asked myself, what did it mean for it to be 'well with my soul' during the worst time of *my* life?

During those seemingly endless times of waiting in hospital, I had cause to reflect on these questions. Through the uncertainty, the heartache, the pain (both physical and emotional) and the longing to be able to take our daughter home with us, my husband and I nonetheless felt ourselves uplifted in prayer. It didn't make everything OK, but the relief of knowing others were lifting us and our situation up to God was palpable. And I was greatly encouraged by Paula Pridham's chapter on prayer, in knowing that my messy, ineloquent prayers were just enough as they were, and that they were being heard by a God who deeply cares for us, in the good times and the bad.

As I pored over the manuscript of this book, I took comfort in the words of the late, great Steve Legg, who speaks of hope and the goodness of God even in the most uncertain of times. And through the writing of Dianne Parsons, I found myself managing to find things (sometimes the very smallest) to be grateful for each day.

As I look at our healthy baby girl, I know that not every hardship has the ending we want. Indeed, each of the authors

---

[2] The Spafford Children's Center 'About Us – History', spaffordcenter.org

in this book have lived experience of both times of struggle and darkness. But they have also experienced the knowledge of God's guiding hand and the assurance of knowing Jesus as the anchor for their souls.

As you read through these beautiful reflections, my hope is that you too will find peace, comfort, hope and so much more.

Jess Hills, Commissioning Editor

CONTENTS

Anchored in Gratitude – Dianne Parsons	9
Anchored in Family – Andy Frost	15
Anchored in Faith – Robin Vincent	23
Anchored in Freedom – Katharine Hill	31
Anchored in Community – Dana Masters	39
Anchored in The Veil – Rob Parsons	47
Anchored in Worship – Lou Fellingham	53
Anchored in Purpose – Mark Chester	63
Anchored in Prayer – Paula Pridham	71
Anchored in Hope – Steve Legg	81
Anchored in Peace – Paul Francis	89

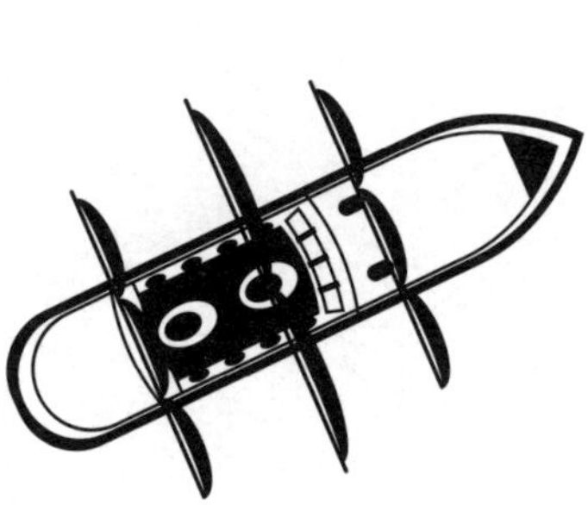

ANCHORED IN GRATITUDE

DIANNE PARSONS

Have you ever heard the saying 'to have an attitude of gratitude'? I read a funny, if a little sad, story recently of two old friends who bumped into each other while out shopping. One of the friends looked tearful, so the other said, 'What in the world has happened to make you so upset?'

The sad friend said, 'Let me tell you. Three weeks ago my long-lost uncle died and left me £40,000.'

'That's a lot of money,' said the friend.

'But then two weeks ago, a cousin of mine died and left me £80,000 and I didn't even know him.'

'Sounds to me like you've been really blessed.'

'But you still don't understand,' he interrupted. 'Last week a great-aunt of mine passed away. I inherited almost £250,000 from her.'

Now the friend was really confused. 'Then why do you look so glum?'

'This week I got nothing!' he said.

I know this is only a story, but it really stuck in my mind – the idea of a person being given these generous gifts and not being grateful, but rather expecting more. That's the thing with receiving something on a regular basis. We eventually come to expect it, and not be appreciative of what we already have.

Gratitude is good for us, and for the people we are grateful to – it feeds our souls.

Recently I sat with a cup of tea and began to wonder ... how much in my life do I take for granted? My home, food, running water, electricity – which includes the internet and TV – among many other things. Sometimes it feels as though I barely notice these things until, suddenly, they don't work. I turn a tap and nothing comes out, or I flick a switch and nothing happens, or worst of all, I point the remote at the TV and the screen doesn't light up! It is only then that I realise how much I depend on these things. This week I needed to dry something quickly and had to pop it in the rarely-used tumble dryer. I pressed the button ... nothing! If I'm honest, I was really frustrated. Just another small example of taking something for granted.

How often do we notice the blessings that God allows us each day? As I watch the devastation of war on the news most days, I realise that my gratitude to God for what I do have is not often shown anything like enough to him. I believe God likes us to be grateful. There's a story in the New Testament where ten men came to Jesus for healing, and He healed them all. Nine of the men went on their way, and only one came back to say thank you. Gratitude is good for us, and for the people we are grateful to – it feeds our soul. And so, in no particular order, I'd like to name some of the things I've found myself most grateful for lately ...

- I love nature – it often moves me to tears. I'm sorry if you think that's dramatic, but it really does. The various colours of the sky, the changing clouds, the multitude of stars at night, and even the different colours of green in the trees. David Attenborough has been brilliant in bringing the deepest of oceans into our living rooms, but it was God who created them.

- I've tried recently to make a habit of thanking God for running water while I clean my teeth. I pray for countries that have to walk miles for a drink, by which time I've long finished cleaning the pearlies. Again, just a small thing, but this prompt helps me to intentionally take time to be grateful for what I often take for granted.

- During the first Covid-19 lockdown, we acquired a black curly colliepoo dog and named her Winnie. We are smitten, and most people who come into contact with her think she's a star – she even smiles at people when they visit! Although it seems silly to some, I'm grateful for the pleasure she brings. I've recently had a few months of ill health, and she's been with me constantly. I am thankful for her being around, and I know she loves when I express this gratitude with pats or treats!

- I adore my family – Rob and I pray and thank God for our children and grandchildren each day. The one thing I do wish though is that they could stay as they are, because as they grow it means I'm getting older – and I'm not enthusiastic about that idea! It also means I have to be more alert when playing board games with my teenage grandchildren, and that's a struggle for me these days. But then I take a moment to be grateful that they still want to play board games with their Nandi, and my heart is light again.

- Some time ago I was out shopping, and I needed to cross a busy main road. As I did, I noticed a young woman with a long stick. While I was able to dash across before the green man flashed, she waited for the peeping sound which told her it was safe to cross. Two things struck me at that moment:
    - That I had vision. Vision to see what was going on around me, and vision to see God's creation that I mentioned earlier. How often do I take that for granted?!
    - Thanks and gratitude for the person who invented the peeping noise at the traffic lights, which is no doubt a life-changer for people with impaired sight.

There you have it – a list of some of the things I am grateful for. And yet there are many more, some of which I probably haven't thought to be grateful for, because I take their presence for granted. This makes me wonder what small daily or weekly habits might help me call attention to these things and consciously be grateful for them, maybe even offering up a prayer of thanks.

Life is busy and often difficult for most of us, and yet for me it seems I can always find time to phone a friend or watch TV, so there must be a time when I could use some of it to be thankful to God for the things I *do* have, however small those things might be. Is it possible to discipline ourselves and build habits that remind us to be grateful? Perhaps when we are showering or washing the dishes, we could pray for local schools – both children and teachers – and the freedom we have in this country. Or we could use the time to pray for friends, family, or the places in the world where others long for the blessings we take for granted.

When we are walking in the park or near the beach, we could remember to thank God for nature and its beauty – not just appreciating it, but redirecting that emotion into gratitude. Even if you can't get out to somewhere like that, being grateful for what's on your doorstep works too. I have a lovely friend called Marilyn, who since she lost her husband often finds solace when she gardens. She says she feels a sense of peace with her Heavenly Father. I'm no gardener, but I do love my garden, and I can remember to be grateful for that.

Is it possible to discipline ourselves and build habits that remind us to be grateful?

Being grateful can help our relationships too. Sadly I think we've lost the art of regularly showing gratitude, so perhaps between us we could revive that dying art. Maybe if we're meeting a friend, we could try to arrive early to show our gratitude to them as a friend. I'm sure it would make us feel better.

There is a wonderful quote that I love, which goes: 'Gratitude turns what we have into enough.' Perhaps if the man who was complaining so bitterly to his friend about not receiving any new riches that week had reflected on the blessings he already had, he would realise that he had enough – and more than enough! When I truly take a look at my life, I realise that I too have enough – and gratitude gives me eyes to see it.

DIANNE PARSONS

Dianne has been involved in the work of Care for the Family since it began in 1988. Over those years she has spoken to thousands of women in events such as *Motherhood – A Rollercoaster Ride, Issues Women Face* and *To Change The Future*. She is the author of two books – *You, Me and Coffee* and *Love, Di*. Dianne is married to Rob and they live in Cardiff. They have two children and five grandchildren.

ANCHORED IN FAMILY

ANDY FROST

When we hear the word 'family', we will all have different images that are conjured up in our minds. In the past week, with this chapter in mind, I have been mulling over the different aspects of family life that are daily noticeable to me, and wanted to share with you a few snapshots from my week ...

> *On Sunday, I am in a restaurant and there is a grandad's 80th birthday party in full motion. He is frail but smiling, donning a 'Birthday Boy' badge with balloons tied meticulously to his chair. The staff line up tables to fit in extended family members, and there is a secondary table for the grandchildren, who are flooding the room with laughter.*

Later in the week, I am on my street walking home and see one of our neighbours, a single mum, taking her three kids to the park. There is tiredness in her posture but a smile on her face as she ushers the kids down the street. They skip alongside her, full of energy and excitement. I greet her as they go past, trying to convey with my eyes and tone what a great job I think she's doing. Her smile lifts a little in response.

On Saturday, we host a BBQ for a few of our kids' school friends and their parents. We are trying to create some normality but there is someone missing. One of the dads recently died. His son and daughter begin to play with the other children. The sadness on their faces is gone for a fleeting moment but it's all still very raw. The mum shares where things are at as the other mums gather around.

The very word 'family' can fill our minds with different pictures, and the truth is, every family is different. Each is unique. The very word has the power to fill us with delight as we cherish what we have and remember happy memories. It may also stir different emotions as we think about the family that we never had or perhaps the family we've lost. In different seasons of life, we may well define family differently.

So with our different experiences, what does it mean to be anchored in family? In my own experience, I have found it to be about the following things ...

Family is a place to be known

For me, the greatest thing about being in a family is that it is real. We live in a world where we can instantly make a connection with new people who don't really know us and very easily reinvent ourselves online, photoshopping our portrait to display who we might want to be, rather than who we really are.

Family members tend to know us more deeply and profoundly than anybody else. My wife can read my emotions better than I can. My mum knows my insecurities and has watched me duel them over the years. My brother has the ability to ask me questions that get to the core of what's going on in my life. And my kids are able to make me laugh when few others can.

At the same time, I know my family members deeply too, from their little idiosyncrasies through to some of the big questions that keep them up at night. This is what can make families a unique space. But because this space is so real and intimate, it can also be challenging. There are those habits that can get on our nerves, the moments when we fail to show each other grace and instead take each other for granted. This is why it is so key to continually show appreciation for the things we love about our family members and to speak about their good qualities.

Family is a place of joy

To be anchored in family is, for me, all about having a sense of joy – in each other, yes, but as a Christian, I like the writer Dallas Willard's description of joy as 'a pervasive sense of wellbeing that is infused with hope because of the goodness of God.'[3] This kind of joy, rooted in God, is one that can stand when hard times come.

We can too often be seduced by the media barrage of what a better life might look like if we were free to do whatever we wanted, whenever we wanted. Or we can compare our family to other families. It's so easy to think that other families have got everything together. But the truth is, no family is perfect. Every family has tensions and misunderstandings and arguments.

---

[3] Dallas Willard, *The Allure of Gentleness: Defending the Faith in the Manner of Jesus* (Bravo Ltd, 2015), p.31.

Being anchored in family is not always easy. It's not all smiles and laughter. There will be seasons to navigate through where life is just really tough. There can be lots of uncertainty about what the future holds. But even in these times, I think we can know the joy of God that Willard speaks about by noticing things to appreciate about our family members.

Family is a place to be thankful

Comparison is a real killer of joy. And on the rollercoaster of family life, giving thanks is vital to combat comparison. Personally, I try and start my times with God by being thankful (as Di shared about in the previous chapter). Sometimes it can be helpful to write down a list of things we are thankful for. I know that I often take too much for granted in family life. This habit helps to rectify that.

I've also tried to make it a habit to say thanks to God as I go about the endless chores of family life. As I drop my kids off at Guides on a wet evening, I am thankful that they have good role models. As I sort the laundry, I am thankful for God's provision of clothes for my family. As I clear away my wife's coffee cups (which seem to breed on her desk!) I am thankful for the fun she brings to our home.

Things go well with my soul when we are thankful as a family.

We try to actively practice thankfulness as a family. When our kids go through all that's in their heads, like the revision that needs doing and the latest computer game they haven't got, my wife is brilliant at asking them, 'What is there to be thankful for?'

Family is a place of prayer

Things go well with my soul when we are thankful as a family. But the Bible also speaks about prayers of petition –

asking God for things. Sometimes, as we look around at our world, we are so aware of the many things that need prayer, and can wonder if God really has time for our small prayer requests. But I love the idea that if something bothers me, then I can bring it to God in prayer.

I try and punctuate my day with short prayers. When my kids were young, I would purposefully pray these prayers out loud, so that they could glimpse the truth of Paul's reminder that we can bring everything to God. I wanted to give my children an insight into how I connect with God in the everyday and bring things to him.

During my childhood, I noticed the high value my parents placed on prayer, and this shaped my view of family life. I would regularly see my dad walk around the local park and pray. I would also see my mum pray for everything from getting a car parking space through to praying for my dad when he was diagnosed with cancer in his 50s.

God doesn't always answer prayers the way we want, but there was something powerful about living in a home saturated in prayer. My dad died at 57, but even in the immediate aftermath of his death, I sensed that we were experiencing the peace of God that the Bible speaks about in that season of grief (Philippians 4:6; John 14:27).

Family is a place to practice kindness

As a family, we try and eat together as often as we can. With two full-time working parents, many dance and gymnastics clubs, and last-minute homework deadlines, it's not always possible. But when we do, we often ask each other the question, 'Where have we seen God at work?'

Responses don't always flow freely, but sometimes we might talk about answered prayer or God-given opportunities to make a difference. The conversation can go anywhere, but I find lots of the words that the Apostle Paul uses in the below passage helpful:

> 'Finally, brothers and sisters, whatever is true, whatever is noble, whatever is right, whatever is pure, whatever is lovely, whatever is admirable – if anything is excellent or praiseworthy – think about such things.'
>
> Philippians 4:8

These words help us think through how we may have seen or demonstrated something of God. For example, one of our kids may have been noble in standing up for another child in the playground, or we may have done the right thing rather than the easy thing in a work situation. It also helps us to think about areas where we could improve.

The simple question 'Was that kind?' is powerful.

It was during these mealtime conversations that we began talking about what makes our family distinctive. What are the values that we want to live by? We would speak about thankfulness, generosity and Christlikeness. One of the key terms the kids latched on to was kindness. And that word has stuck.

It has been one of those words that we have used to keep each other accountable in family life. The simple question, 'Was that kind?' has been powerful, especially when our kids now ask it of us!

Now, my kids aren't perfect, but at my 12-year-old daughter's dance show, she was mentioned at the very end. In the packed auditorium with 250 children, and many more parents and carers, she was given the 'Kindness Award'. Proud dad moment! It is within our family that this value has been fostered, and my hope and prayer is that in the changing seasons of life, she will continue to be known for her kindness.

Family is a place to reflect God's goodness

In among Paul's words in Philippians 4:8 are two words that are a bit out of the ordinary. Interestingly, the words 'lovely' and 'admirable' aren't used anywhere else in the New Testament. These words aren't about faith and morality. They are words about inherent beauty. Theologians describe them in terms of common grace – signs of the goodness of God in culture.

When people preach on thought patterns, we can often focus on what we shouldn't be watching or consuming, but I love that Paul spins it the other way. Paul, despite being in chains, is encouraging us to focus on what is good in the world.

We live in challenging times and our news headlines are pretty desperate. While it is important to engage with injustice in the world – praying for victims, giving generously, petitioning government and doing what we can in our community – the heaviness of the world can take its toll. It helps my soul, and I'm sure those of others, to think on and seek out what is good.

For us as a family with young kids, this can look like intentionally pointing out and celebrating the good things – short videos of cute animals, the latest dance craze, the colours of the sunset and the taste of homemade cake. I want to help my kids see what is good, to notice and celebrate it. It is so important to both be grateful for our blessings and pray for those who don't have the same, making our family a place of thankfulness and prayer.

As my kids begin the move from primary school to secondary, I am all too aware that the years really do fly by.

My understanding of family will continue to evolve. It's never static and there is always lots of uncertainty about what the future holds. But if Paul, chained up in prison, uncertain if he would be executed, managed to write all about joy, then I want to choose joy for my family.

Family life is both hard work and a real privilege. Whatever family life looks like for you, whether you are an 80-year-old grandad or a single parent, I hope these reflections will be an encouragement to you. There is so much to be anxious about, but in my family, we are choosing prayer laced with thankfulness, and to dwell on the goodness of God.

ANDY FROST

Andy loves adventures – over the years he has run ultra-marathons, surfed big waves, and wing-walked at 12,000 feet. However, he believes that the greatest adventure is following Jesus. He is director of Share Jesus International, a popular speaker, and author of several books, including *Raising Faith* and *52 Faith Adventures for Dads and Their Kids*. Andy is married to Jo and they have two young adventurers, Eloise and Talitha.

ANCHORED IN FAITH

ROBIN VINCENT

In the summer of 2024, I fell off my mountain bike, breaking my leg and tearing my ligaments. While I knew that my ego and injuries would both heal, the discomfort and inconvenience still affected me and those around me. In my capacity as CEO of Care for the Family, I was due to tour with one of our parenting events and had many other planned speaking engagements in the diary – all of which had to be cancelled or rearranged. As if that weren't enough, my kind and patient wife Hannah suddenly found her workload dramatically increased in order to look after me during my recovery!

Aside from my accident illustrating how suddenly life can change, I am aware that by comparison, it is somewhat insignificant and trivial to what others are facing. For example, last week Hannah and I received news of the sudden loss of a friend. He was more than just our friend, though. We would describe him as one of life's good guys, and his humble, kind and servant-hearted nature made him an inspiration and example to many who knew him. In all honesty, his loss felt far too soon and entirely wrong.

> **The anchor that holds our little boat steady is God's faithfulness, rather than ours.**

Yet the disciple James wrote that we will all face trials and troubles of many kinds (James 1:2), and I get the sense he is saying that they all matter. While some circumstances are undoubtedly worse than others, I am not sure how helpful it is in the midst of a storm to try and rank what we are experiencing as either more or less trivial or tragic. Whenever and however our lives are disrupted, whether it be for a short time or far longer, it is natural for us to feel unsettled or uncertain in our faith. Thankfully though, the anchor that holds our little boat steady (or at least keeps it afloat) is God's faithfulness, rather than ours. This is the certainty we need when everything else may seem uncertain. Contemplating trouble, hardship or even death is not as depressing as never having thought about them at all. Consequently, it is good for us to dwell on the question of where we find this certainty.

The gospel writer Luke began his account of Jesus' life by expressing his desire that the reader would know the certainty of the things they had been taught (Luke 1:3). This certainty also characterises the stories of the 'great crowd of witnesses' we see described in Hebrews 12:1. They were not held steady by their circumstances, but by their confidence and hope in something better that had yet to come. Paul encourages us to get our certainty from the good news of Christ, and to remember that those things written about in the past are for our encouragement, so we might have confidence and hope. This is especially important when life is less enjoyable and demands that we demonstrate endurance. It is in those times that the certainties of our faith help us trust God's heart even when we cannot trace his hand.

The pastor Dietrich Bonhoeffer certainly had to grapple with this. While sitting in a Gestapo prison cell a few days before Christmas 1943, he wrote to a friend saying, 'I must be able to know for certain that I am in the hands of God, not in men's.'[4] By April 1945 he had been moved to a concentration camp. Early one morning, he was stripped of his clothes, and along with several others led to the place of execution. Just before he began that walk to the gallows he reportedly said to a fellow prisoner, 'This is the end, but for me it is the beginning of life.'

This is the same certainty demonstrated by the late pastor and leader of the Evangelical Alliance, Joel Edwards, who wrote a final letter to his friends across the world in June 2021, saying: 'I have gone home. My earnest prayer is that your faith and tenacity on my behalf will not be considered a pointless religious exercise, but that it will have strengthened your faith in a God who is marvellous, mysterious and majestic in all that He does: The Faithful One ... I wait to welcome you.'[5]

In the book *Safely Home*, a fictional story of the persecuted church, there are two central characters, Ben and Quan. The former lives in the United States and the latter in China.

---

4 Dietrich Bonhoeffer, *Letters And Papers From Prison* (Fontana, 1968), p.60.

5 Kelly Valencia, 'Tributes to "hero of the faith" Joel Edwards who has died from cancer', *Premier Christian News*, 30 June 2021 [accessed 19 July 2024].

Both are Christians, but Quan's life of faith is lived out within a hostile environment. As their friendship develops, Ben becomes increasingly aware of Quan's challenges and says to him:

> "When I see what you've been going through, I think about my brother-in-law. He attends a big church in California. For years he told Pam and me, 'If you serve God, you'll be healthy and prosperous."
>
> 'In China it is the opposite. You may be healthy and prosperous before you are a Christian. But once you start serving God, seldom will you stay that way.'
>
> 'Well, maybe a gospel that's true in California but not in China isn't the true gospel.'
>
> 'My friend has made a proverb. Very wise.'
>
> 'You have to have hope, Quan. Don't you think things will get better?'
>
> 'They will. But in this world? That, we cannot know. Our hope is in another world." [6]

Dietrich Bonhoeffer, Joel Edwards and Quan all serve to remind me that the certainty I need to keep me steady in the storms is not only eternal in nature, but it must also be true in every context, country and century. In other words, the faith we have must make sense wherever we are, whatever is happening, and in whatever age we live. Anything less may not be the real deal.

Several years ago, Hannah and I were travelling in the United States, and we came across an unusual business called The Zombie Apocalypse shop. This was no party shop – it was the real deal! We managed to muster up sufficient courage

---

[6] Randy Alcorn, *Safely Home* (Tyndale House, 2011), p.323.

to step inside. I want you to imagine the kind of man you would want by your side if you were facing a pack of zombies. That is what the owner of the shop looked like – he was quite intimidating. Unsurprisingly, the shop was not particularly busy, and so we got into conversation with the owner. He sold weapons and survival paraphernalia, and so it felt a little foolish (albeit honest) to admit to him that we were not going to buy anything and were merely visiting out of curiosity.

As the conversation wore on, I grew in confidence that he would let us out alive, and this led me to be brave enough to ask him, 'You don't really believe in zombies, do you?' I have never forgotten his reply: 'Define what you mean by zombie.' In other words, this shop was not about preparing to deal with the walking dead, but about preparing for trouble ahead. He was a prepper, and while my first instinct was to laugh off his perspective, it struck me that we should all be preppers. Granted, not in the way this guy was, but rather in the way Jesus described when he said, 'Lay up for yourselves treasure in heaven' (Matthew 6:20). This shop owner spoke about what he thought was coming with a certainty that was evident by his actions. The certainty of our faith – the promise of something better tomorrow – must have a similar effect upon us today.

C. S. Lewis touched on something akin to this when he wrote to encourage his friend, Mary Neyland. He acknowledged that confidence in what we believe to be true does not always come naturally, comparing it to the act of swimming: '[I]n learning to swim you believe, and even know intellectually that water will support you long before you feel any real confidence in the fact.'[7] Therefore, in learning to swim we

[7] C. S. Lewis, *Collected Letters Volume Two: Books, Broadcasts and War, 1931–1949* (HarperCollins Publishers, 2004), Kindle Edition, location 10631.

have to act in a manner that is sometimes contrary to how we feel. Lewis reflects '... we will only develop faith by acting as if we already have it'[8] because as James reminded the early Christians, it is by our actions that our faith is made complete. In the same letter, Lewis observes that falls, failure and other disappointments will inevitably happen, but encourages Mary that 'we shall of course be very muddy and tattered children by the time we reach home. But the bathrooms are all ready, the towels put out, and the clean clothes are in the airing cupboard'.[9]

Last autumn I was on tour with Care for the Family. I had just arrived at the church venue for the evening event, when I received a phone call from Hannah. She was ringing to update me on my mum, who had been admitted to hospital a few days earlier. Hannah had spoken to the doctors, and it was clear that my mother was not long for this world. Upon entering the vestry, which had been set aside as a pre-event room for the speakers, I noticed that the church members had left me a gift. It was a holding cross – a small wooden cross designed to fit comfortably in the palm of one's hand. This was not something I had come across before, but I was told that they are often used as a source of comfort and physical connection for those who are suffering. If I am honest, it felt like a gift from God himself.

I returned home almost immediately, and when I visited my mum in the hospital she was barely conscious, but I lifted the blankets and placed the holding cross firmly in her hand. She held that cross for the next three days before she passed away on the Sunday. As I drove away from the hospital, it struck me that the faith my mother had was not in how sincerely or firmly she held onto that cross in her final hours.

---

[8] Ibid.

[9] Ibid.

Rather, it was in the certainty and faithfulness of the one who hung on the cross in his final hours. In other words, it was not how firm she felt her faith was, but how firmly God was holding on to her. He was the anchor of her faith, holding her steady in the final storm.

In the days leading up to his own death, Jesus said a fascinating thing to his disciples: 'My sheep listen to my voice; I know them, and they follow me. I give them eternal life, and they shall never perish; no one will snatch them out of *my hand*. My Father, who has given them to me, is greater than all, no one can snatch them out of *my Father's hand*' (John 10:27-29, emphasis mine). He was speaking about the certainty of the grip of God upon our lives, and the good news is that it is a double-handed grip.

We are not home yet, but our certainty is that one day we will be.

During his final hours, Jesus reminded his disciples, 'I have told you these things so that in me you may have peace. In this world you will have trouble, but take heart, for I have overcome the world' (John 16:33). Trouble and death are awful realities, but the faithfulness of Christ means both have lost their sting. In the midst of the complexity and mystery that Good Friday and Easter Sunday bring, we also find the gift of certainty. We are not home yet, but our certainty is that one day we will be. On that day, whenever it might be, our arrival will not be a surprise. The Father will be waiting. As we reach the door of the Father's house we will discover Christ's key was in the lock all the time. We shall then cross the threshold with confidence and discover a room that has been prepared for us. Upon the bed will be a crown, a ring, a robe and shoes intended for a child that has returned home at last.

In Charlotte Brontë's novel *Jane Eyre*, the heroine Jane comforts her friend Helen in the final days of a terminal illness. She asks Helen:

> "Are you going somewhere, Helen? Are you going home?'
> 'Yes; to my long home – my last home." [10]

On earth all our books will include pages of loss, disappointment, heartache and struggle. Most likely these will be placed among other moments of joy, laughter and celebration. However, the latter rarely make the former any easier. Yet by faith we have invited the most faithful character in history into our story. Even better than that, we have the certainty that we have been written into his bigger and better story. At the end of our days on earth, we will discover that what was said of the four children in Narnia is also true for us:

> 'All their life in this world and all their adventures had only been the cover and the title page: now at last they were beginning Chapter One of the Great Story which no one on earth has read: which goes on for ever: in which every chapter is better than the one before.' [11]

ROBIN VINCENT

Robin is the chief executive of Care for the Family. He has over two decades of experience in pastoral leadership, as well as holding leadership roles in the private, public and third sector. He and his wife Hannah have two children and live in Swansea.

---

[10] Charlotte Brontë, *Jane Eyre: The Original 1847 Unabridged and Complete Edition* (Global Publishers, 2023), p.100.
[11] C. S. Lewis, *The Last Battle* (HarperCollins, 1997), p.172.

ANCHORED IN FREEDOM

KATHARINE HILL

It was my first day at boarding school. The journey seemed to have taken an age, but finally there I was, standing on the steps, waving goodbye to my family. In my left hand I held my bag, and in my right hand, my teddy bear. I was ten years old.

I watched the tail lights of the car disappear down the drive, and taking a deep breath, went inside to this strange new world. Later that night, I lay in my bed in the darkness and wondered what the next day would bring. I held my teddy close; he was a shabby little bear with much of his fur loved off. Just as I was drifting off to sleep the matron put her head around the door. 'Girls,' she said. 'Sarah in the next room is crying because she's missing home. I wondered if anyone might have a spare teddy she could borrow?'

I agonised for a moment, but it didn't take me long to decide. As I handed over my precious bear, I felt the warm glow of satisfaction that often comes with a sacrificial act of giving. I felt sad for Sarah and was pleased my teddy might bring her some comfort. But in that split second, something else happened; something much deeper, something I would not be aware of for decades. I made the unconscious decision that I was never going to be Sarah. I would never admit to missing home or be vulnerable enough to say I needed a teddy.

I put on the strong, protective armour of self-sufficiency which served me well, and I set out to prove myself to my new friends, to the school, and to my parents. My ten-year-old ambition over the next seven years was to achieve three things: to earn a much-coveted place in the school choir, a place in the 1st team for sports, and most of all, a place in the hallowed 'Study One' – home to the Head Girl, Deputy Head Girl and Captain of Games. And over the years that followed, I set my mind to those tasks and did them well. And it felt so good.

Perhaps as a way to navigate the challenges of boarding school, it wasn't a bad strategy. But as I came to discover, striving to live in the well-worn groove of achievement and success as a 20-, 30-, 40-, even 50-something is not sustainable. In fact it often caused me to burn the candle at both ends.

As a young lawyer, I'd rehearse my performance until the early hours the night before a hearing. As a young mother, I'd stay up way too late putting the finishing touches on birthday cakes or World Book Day costumes. The need to achieve and excel propelled me across the finishing tape in the mothers' race, saw me relegating my sunken Victoria sponge or less-than-perfect chocolate brownies to the bin, and even drove me to rehearse eloquent prayers for the student committee prayer meeting.

For so many of us, the adrenaline rush of success and achievement massages our ego and appeals to our sense of importance, so that gradually we come to believe that our worth and value lies in what we do. Living *for* rather than *from* approval, we find ourselves responding to an exhausting litany of 'oughts' and 'shoulds', and before we know it, we are tethered to this powerful source of identity and worth, which does damage to our souls.

Living from a need to prove ourselves can drive us to overcommit and live our lives in a persistent state of busyness. As a black-suited, kitten-heeled lawyer by day, a denim-clad, music-loving, coffee-drinking youth group leader by night, and the 'hostess-with-the-mostest' at weekends, I made every second count. The arrival of children saw the kitten heels exchanged for trainers and the black suit for a banana-stained T-shirt, but essentially the pace of life remained the same. In the years that followed, what the Bible calls the 'worries of life' (Mark 4:19) – aka all that is involved in parenting four lively children: Saturday sports fixtures, school parents' evenings, searching for missing hamsters and swimming goggles, all while fighting the losing battle of a half-tidy house – were making their presence felt. At that time, I was church warden of a big Anglican church, a role which required not only time and energy, but considerable emotional and

> **As I read the Bible, I don't notice words like 'efficiency' or 'productivity' describing the way of Jesus.**

spiritual investment. I had pressed the pause button on my role as a solicitor, but I was hearing cases and seeking to deliver justice as a magistrate.

Putting on a hero's cape means you can cover a lot of ground and get stuff done. But as time went on, I began to have a nagging feeling that my outward productivity was a smokescreen for a restlessness in my soul, and that there had to be something more. Multitasking gave the illusion that I could achieve and perform well, without giving my full attention to anything. On the surface, everything was good and worthwhile – there was just too much of it. Life was wide but not very deep. As I read the Bible, I didn't notice words like 'efficiency' or even 'productivity' describing the way of Jesus.

The Bible is full of examples of people whose lives were marked by striving and effort. In Exodus, we read that Moses sat as judge for the people, who stood around from morning to night waiting for him to adjudicate their cases. He was going it alone, and he was exhausted. It took a visit from his father-in-law Jethro to help him see the folly of his ways: 'What you are doing is not good. You and these people ... will only wear yourselves out. The work is too heavy for you; you cannot handle it alone' (Exodus 18:17–18). He challenged Moses to take off his Superman cape, admit he couldn't be all things to all people, and delegate some of his responsibilities to others.

It is a paradox in the Christian life that when we are anchored in the freedom that Christ gives us, we learn to live within limits. Ruth Haley Barton reflects on how, in the New Testament, Paul grapples honestly with the reality of limitations:

> 'When [Paul] wrote about not thinking more highly of ourselves than we ought (Romans 12:3), he was making

> a very general statement about limiting our grandiosity and pride by cultivating a realistic sense of our essential nature. He was talking about being willing to live within the limits and the possibilities of who we really are … Living within limits is not in any way an acquiescence that is despairing, passive, or fatalistic. Rather it honors the deepest realities of the life God has given us. Life in this body at this age and stage. Life in our family at its age and stage. Life in this personality. Life with this community. Life in the midst of this calling.' [12]

I still have a long way to go, but I have found moments of unexpected freedom when I have learnt to live and work within accepting my limitations. This was a lesson often learnt the hard way. My husband Richard and I enjoy offering hospitality, in particular sharing good food, good conversation and relaxed space around the kitchen table. But during an especially busy season, I found this was taking a toll on me. I was confused. I usually love cooking and welcoming people into our home – so why was I finding it so unmanageable and utterly exhausting? In his goodness, God sent a 'Jethro' my way with the loving challenge: 'What you are doing is not good. You will only wear yourself out.' My Jethro encouraged me to consider what hospitality meant for us within the boundaries and limits of this season of our lives. She explained that hospitality required not just physical and social energy (which I had in abundance), but also carried an emotional and spiritual cost, which for me at that time was sorely depleted. I realised that I had slipped into thinking that as a 'good Christian' I should always have an open house and had simply ploughed ahead, without acknowledging the limitations of what I was able to do at that particular time. On

[12] Ruth Haley Barton, *Strengthening the Soul of Your Leadership: Seeking God in the Crucible of Ministry* (InterVarsity Press, 2018), pp.109, 112.

this occasion, laying down the striving and recognising the finiteness of what I could do brought me a freedom I hadn't previously known.

Striving perfectionism is not the way of Jesus. The need to prove ourselves is a trap that prevents us going deeper into the transforming presence of God, and experiencing the freedom that that brings. It is the antithesis of the way Jesus lived.

Bookending the accounts of Jesus' ministry are two stories that bear witness to the fact that here was a man who had nothing to prove. Right at the beginning of his ministry, Jesus goes to John to be baptised. The Bible tells us that heaven was opened, the Spirit of God descended like a dove and alighted on him, and a voice from heaven proclaimed: 'This is my Son, whom I love; with him I am well pleased' (Matthew 3:17). Jesus hadn't yet told a parable or performed a single miracle – and the Father was pleased with him. Straight away, Jesus is led by the Spirit into the desert to be tempted by the devil. Satan opens by playing what he believes is a trump card; he calls into question Jesus' very identity: '*If* you are the Son of God ... ' (Matthew 4:3, my emphasis). But it is this identity that has just been affirmed by Jesus' Father, and, secure in it, Jesus stands firm.

It is as we keep company with Jesus and seek to walk with the Spirit that we become anchored in freedom.

Fast forward just three years and the apostle John invites us to accompany Jesus during the last week of his life. It was just before the Passover Feast, and the evening meal was being served. John writes:

> 'Jesus knew that the Father had put all things under his power, and that he had come from God and was returning to God; so he got up from the meal, took off his outer

> clothing, and wrapped a towel round his waist. After that, he poured water into a basin and began to wash his disciples' feet, drying them with the towel that was wrapped round him.'
>
> John 13:3–5

In his life on earth, Jesus lived *from* and not *for* the Father's approval. He was totally secure in his identity. And he came to offer us that same freedom and security. Paul writes in Galatians that 'It is for freedom that Christ has set us free' (5:1). We don't have to live imprisoned in a way of life that demands our continual striving to prove ourselves, either to God or to others. Yes, we will want to continue making every effort to serve him, but we will do so knowing that his yoke is easy to bear. It is our willingness to serve him that matters to him most, not our success or failure.

When we know deep down the freedom that Jesus has given us, we can make the most of opportunities that come our way, and give our best without wearing ourselves out in the process. As we begin to lay down our striving and relinquish the need to prove our worth, we will create space for God to remind us of his unconditional love for us. Our identity is secure in him. The first step is to remind ourselves that 'there is nothing I can do to make God love me more and nothing I can do to make him love me less.'[13] We have nothing to prove. Our anchor is secure.

Jesus says:

> 'I'll show you how to take a real rest. Walk with me and work with me – watch how I do it. Learn the unforced rhythms of grace ... Keep company with me and you'll learn to live freely and lightly.'
>
> Matthew 11:28–30, MSG

[13] Philip Yancey, *What's So Amazing About Grace?* (Harper Collins, 2023), p.70.

It is as we keep company with Jesus and seek to walk with the Spirit, attentive to his presence in our everyday lives that we become anchored in freedom. It is a place where our sins are forgiven, where our burdens are light; it is a place of connection and intimacy with the Father; a place where we have nothing to prove.

If left unchecked, my personality will default to performance. But I am grateful that as I seek to lay down the striving and find time to be attentive to the love of God in me and around me, that I will experience the deep joy of knowing that it is indeed 'well with my soul.'

KATHARINE HILL

Katharine is a director of Care for the Family and a popular speaker, writer and broadcaster. She has practised as a family lawyer and served as a board member for the International Commission on Couple and Family Relations. She is the author of several books, including *Born Free: A Call to be Still, Know God and Flourish in a Hectic World*. Katharine and her husband Richard live in Bristol, and they have four children and seven grandchildren.

ANCHORED IN COMMUNITY

DANA MASTERS

It's Sunday morning and I am ten years old. I'm waking up in Granny's house and the smell of her cooking is already filling the space all around me. My granny wore many hats but perhaps her most impressive, at least to the outside world, was that of civil rights activist. In fact, she was so instrumental in justice work in our home state of South Carolina that they recently named a highway after her. But to me this morning, this legend of a woman is just my granny, the chef.

I roll over, torn between the warm comfort of Granny's guest bed and the blissful domesticity of her kitchen. I can hear pots on the boil and the telephone ringing off the hook with all the community's needs and goings-on, still demanding her attention. I hear the *snick* of Granny's knife as she chops vegetables, the *sploosh* as she stirs with her wooden spoon, and the happy buzz of conversation as she prepares for the arrival of our family. As I inhale the delicious scent of her legendary Sunday lunch, the excitement of what's to come eventually propels me out of bed.

Today is full of my favourites: getting dressed in my Sunday best, going to church with PopPop at St. Mount Olive Baptist Church, riding there in his old classic American car, the delight of playing with my cousins and welcoming any extra souls needing a family. Best of all ... enjoying Granny's cooking! I am overwhelmed with anticipation and joy. I feel like the luckiest girl in the whole world!

Granny's table was a second home to me. It was the first place I truly belonged; the place I felt most myself. And it was all because of the people gathered around her table – my people, my family. My Mama, my PopPop, my uncles, aunties and cousins; they were my very first community. They were the first place I received a sense of identity. It was around that table where I was baptised in the stories of our past and the hopes for our future. It was around that table that I was taught of our collective need for Jesus, a Saviour larger than us and the problems we faced. And it was at this table I learned to take comfort and find joy in being together even when all else seemed unsure and terrifying.

The funny thing is, I am not a people person. I mean, I am, but I'm also not. That is to say, my people love me. I am fun to be around. I am entertaining and caring. I am funny; I love making people laugh. It means a great deal to me that they feel valued in my presence and people enjoy that about me. And I genuinely enjoy making them feel good. But it costs me. Quite a lot, actually, because I am a true introvert – I need time alone and in solitude to energise myself. But when I was growing up, being together as often as possible was a non-negotiable. Taking part in special meals, sitting at the table and engaging in meaningful conversation was expected of us as children.

Looking back, I can see now that it was intentional; more than just a bit of fun. Our parents and grandparents knew firsthand just how hard life could be. So many of my family members grew up in the Jim Crow South[14] – my grandmother's children were the first children in their county to desegregate the school system. They knew that the journey in front of us would be hard and unpredictable at times, with most of what would happen around us out of our control and we would need a safe place, an anchor. And so, around this table, they were doing the hard work of planting us. My Granny, my PopPop, my Mama and my aunts, as imperfect as they were, set about this holy task: taking our tiny fragile roots and burying them deep in the soil of all they had to give – a legacy of faith, love and courage. They showed us how to need each other and how to show up for each other. They taught us to listen and to laugh and find joy in one another, even when life was throwing its worst at us. They instilled in us that whatever may come, we would never walk it alone. It wasn't perfect, but it was powerful.

It's Sunday morning and I am 41 years old. I'm still an introvert. I'm waking up in my home in Northern Ireland, a long way from Granny's table and the family I love deeply. If I want to smell soul food wafting throughout my home, I have to make it. If I want to feel that sense of belonging on this side of the world, I have to build it.

---

[14] This term refers to the set of discriminatory laws that enforced racial segregation in the US between 1877-1950.

As I come to after a long sleep, all of life's worries crowd in, clamouring and demanding, sitting heavily on my mind and heart. And so the weekly internal debate ensues: 'I'm exhausted. How did the weekend pass so quickly with hardly a whiff of rest? Why did I plan this Sunday lunch? Why did I invite guests? Do you think they'd mind terribly if I cancelled?' Then, 'I can't cancel. I've been preparing that chicken for 48 hours!'

And so I peel my tired body from the comfort of my warm bed to put the kettle on. I preheat the oven so that the chicken I've been brining for the last two days will be slowly roasted while we are at church. I mentally go through my checklist for this labour-intensive meal I decided to make. The carrots are chopped, the vegetable trivet prepped, potatoes peeled, marinade mixed, serving dishes and plates wiped down and put in the warming oven ... and so on.

These are the moments I clear my heart of its natural selfishness to make room for the beautiful work of Christ in my home.

Any moment now the house will be bathed in the sounds of chaotic family life, but right now all is still quiet, and these few moments are mine alone.

So while the coffee brews in the French press, I clear the dining table of all the signs of life that gather throughout the week. Immediately I feel a bit more alive. This is my favourite part. As I get out the linen tablecloth and the matching napkins and begin to arrange them on the table, I can feel their presence here. My family. Their laughter and stories, guiding me as I do the work of cultivating the soil for my own children's roots to be buried deep in.

It's hard work. Sometimes it feels back-breaking as I contort myself, my life, and my busy schedule to make room for this holy calling. It's never convenient or easy. But I know deep in my soul that it is essential. So here I am – tiredly, imperfectly cultivating community the only way I know how. Granny's way. This preparation, this sacrifice; this is all part of it. These are the moments I die to self and clear my heart of its natural selfishness to make room for the beautiful work of Christ in my home.

I strive away from making this work performative, done so that people can see and think me amazing, the perfect pastor's wife with the well-kept house and well-made table. No, I actively keep it transformative, so that the folks who know my inner life and my story, who walk with me through difficult times, will see the effort I made for us and feel valued, loved and seen.

I move through my home, preparing to receive our family, our friends, and sometimes new friends in need of a safe place. Today they will come, burdened with their own chaos and fears; their own needs and disappointments. I progress through my to-do list; every motion of preparation a prayer over the effort:

> 'Jesus, I lay this table in the same way you lay a table before us. In the presence of all that seeks to terrify and destroy us, we, the imperfect and unworthy, feast, laugh and hope. Would you come? Make your home here among us. Plant our roots deep so when the storms come we will be OK.'

I've come a long way from Granny's table in South Carolina. I have grown, evolved and changed since my time at that table. But my roots remain in the soil of those meals with those people around that table. They remain my 'great cloud of witnesses' (Hebrews 12:1). They cheer me on, some from the other side of eternity, as I fumble my way through doing the same for my family and friends.

Cultivating community is essential for a life well lived. And it is for all of us, regardless of culture, personality or culinary ability! It can happen around a table laid with the most exquisite Sunday lunch, or a table of pizza served on paper plates. But there is something deeply and profoundly miraculous that happens when we break bread together regularly with open hearts. This work is a gift, a tool for us from heaven. I have learnt that my life is only as strong as the village around me, and that village's foundation is built upon tables.

Want to know a secret? I have no felt need for other people. I know! Sounds crazy to say it after I've harped on about community! My introversion is such that I rarely *feel* the desire to be with others. But not *feeling* a need and not having a need are two very different things. I have no felt need for exercise – I know I'm not alone on this one! But I *know* I need it. My need for it is not based on my feelings; it's based on the way I was created to function. And so I do it (begrudgingly most of the time!) and my mind and body thank me for it. The same is true for me with community. My need for it is not based on my feelings, but it is rooted in the way I was created. And we were created for community. It's as simple as that. If you want to live a life that is full and rich, you must live it in community.

It's 8.00pm. Sunday lunch is over and our guests have all gone home in preparation for the week ahead. I have sent my children off to prepare for bed and I'm staring at the utter carnage of the table after our full Sunday lunch. Back in my kitchen, alone again (my happy place), I reflect on the day. Grateful that I didn't follow my feelings and cancel, I feel full of something warm and lovely. I pause to try and identify the sentiment.

As I take a moment, I remember when at the height of the chaos I looked out onto my own table and saw it overflowing with people, food, laughter, conversations and love, and I know exactly what this warm ball in my chest is. It's the sweet pleasure and presence of God. It's knowing, deep in my bones, that a good work was done here. We all left that table a little stronger, a little more joyful, a little less alone.

I have learnt that my life is only as strong as the village around me, and that village's foundation is built upon tables.

As I prepare to reorder the chaos all around me, I see it as the evidence of the seeds of community budding right here, in my home. This is the work of community; of anchoring yourself to others, no matter how imperfect or inconvenient. With every dish I rinse and pack into the dishwasher, I breathe out my prayers: 'Thank you for it all, Lord. Thank you.'

When the kitchen is once again put to rights, I make my way to bed, pausing at my children's rooms to kiss them goodnight. I'm wrecked, bone tired, but overflowing with thankfulness and hope. And the old hymn weaves its way through my heart: 'Whatever my lot, Thou hast taught me to say, it is well, it is well with my soul.'

DANA MASTERS

Dana is a professional jazz singer and TV presenter. She and her husband Andrew live on a wild mountain in Northern Ireland and have three children. They worship at Lagan Valley Vineyard Church where Andrew is a church leader.

ANCHORED IN THE VEIL

ROB PARSONS

It is impossible to read the story of Horatio Spafford without asking the question, 'Why do bad things happen to good people?' It seems that in general, the human race finds that question one of the most perplexing dilemmas in the universe; yet it is not a surprise to God. The oldest book in the Bible, the book of Job, tackles that very issue in a most dramatic fashion. How will Job's love for God hold up when it seems that God is not keeping his end of the bargain?

The honest truth is that suffering of all kinds – whether great like that of the Spaffords, or sometimes of a much less significant nature – can cause us to question God's love for us.

Listen in to Bart Simpson's prayer life. It's Christmas Eve. 'O God, if you bring me lots of good stuff tomorrow, I promise not to do anything bad between now and when I wake up.'

Bart's deal with God may make us smile, but it may make us think as well. Could it be that unwittingly we are living our lives with the unspoken belief that we have a secret 'deal' with God? It goes something like this:

> 'God, I will follow you, serve and love you, but in return you will look after me. A little pain, some persecution that doesn't get too nasty, and minor family traumas are all accepted as part of my sanctification. But that's it. No failing marriages, children who turn their backs on church, illnesses that kill those I love, or redundancies that don't ultimately lead to a more fulfilling job.'

I remember a man in his mid-40s. He had been a Christian for years and had seemed to live a charmed life. He had a lovely home, a wonderful family, was financially secure and had been given talent in abundance. Tom was good at everything. Then one day he was made redundant. But his job wasn't the only thing he lost that day. Tom lost his faith in God. He has never been inside a church since. He said to a friend, 'If there is a God who loves me, he wouldn't have let this happen to me.'

Don't be too hard on him. You and I may not know how we will react when we experience what one theologian referred to as 'the seeming betrayal of God'.

I suppose it's in the book of Habakkuk that we find the most eloquent summary of the idea of holding on to faith in God when life turns bad on us:

> 'Though the fig tree does not bud
> and there are no grapes on the vines,

> though the olive crop fails
> and the fields produce no food,
> though there are no sheep in the pen
> and no cattle in the stalls,
> yet I will rejoice in the Lord,
> I will be joyful in God my Saviour.'

Habakkuk 3:17–18

I find it hard to read that passage because it makes me ask myself whether I love God like that. Secretly, do I only love him if he seems to be good to me?

Life can change in a moment. I experienced that ten years ago on a sunny September morning. My daughter Katie was in hospital after having a routine procedure and I rang her to see how she was doing. She said, 'I don't feel well, Dad.' Those five words ushered in a period in my life that I will never forget. The simple operation had gone wrong and within hours Katie was rushed back into the operating theatre. Over the next few days, she had two major operations and it looked as though her very life hung by a thread.

You and I may not know how we will react when we experience 'the seeming betrayal of God'.

Katie and her husband Paul have two children, and when Paul was looking after them and couldn't be at her bedside, I took his place – often sitting for hours just watching her sleeping, with tubes seemingly coming out of every part of her body. Dianne had gone in for a hip replacement operation the day before Katie was admitted, so she too was in hospital – albeit a different one, 15 miles away.

When I visited Dianne we would talk together, but Katie couldn't do that. I don't like sitting still, yet I found it strangely easy to simply be by that bedside, watching her and praying.

Over the years, I have seen life traumas affect people's faith in such different ways. Some have said, as Tom, the man I mentioned above, did: 'There can't be a God who loves me. If there was, he wouldn't let me go through this.' I understand that reaction.

Another reaction is a bit less clear-cut, and goes something like this: 'I don't really understand any of this. I know that if you said just one word you could put it all right this very second, though I also know that doesn't always happen. But whatever does happen, I need you more than ever. Please make this terror go away, but in it, and through it, and even if the very worst happens, please hold me in this darkness.'

Mine was the second reaction. I don't think it was because I am any more spiritual than others who had the first response. It is simply that as I sat by Katie's bed, I realised that it all came down to one simple question: 'Do I trust God to somehow keep holding us all – whatever happens?' And I discovered that I did. That discovery was almost a surprise – a bit like the old poet in the Psalms saying, 'If I go up to the heavens, you are there. If I make my bed in the depths, you are there ... even there ... your right hand will hold me fast.' (Psalm 139:8–10). In other words, 'I really didn't expect to find you *here!*'

In my heart, I know that real love doesn't operate on the basis of a deal.

In the middle of this experience, I had to address our staff at one of our conferences. I shared my sadness and worry at Katie's illness and spoke about a verse from the book of Hebrews which says, 'We have this hope as an anchor for the soul, firm and secure' (Hebrews 6:19). I mentioned that in sailing, what is often of most importance is not the size of the anchor, but what the anchor is sunk into. The writer to the Hebrews reminded followers of Jesus who were going through the most difficult of times that their security lay in the very strength of God.

A few days after the conference, I was looking after Katie and Paul's son Harry for the afternoon. He was just four years old. As we walked along, hand in hand, he was singing to himself a song he had learned in Sunday school. I said to him, 'Hey Harry, you seem to know that song really well. Would you sing it for me?'
He smiled. 'Sure, Pops.'

The second he started, I knew something special was going on and I captured it on my phone. As his mother lay fighting for her life in hospital, this little boy sang to his grandfather the worship song *Cornerstone:*

> *My hope is built on nothing less*
> *than Jesus' blood and righteousness.*
> *I dare not trust the sweetest frame,*
> *but wholly trust in Jesus' name.*
>
> *Christ alone, Cornerstone,*
> *weak made strong in the Saviour's love.*
> *Through the storm,* (head lifted to the sky in one of the actions he'd been taught!)
> *He is Lord,*
> *Lord of all.*

As I turned off the camera and hugged him, I had tears streaming down my face. From the lips of a child, I was told that my hope is built on something solid – a cornerstone, or in the words of Hebrews 'an anchor for the soul.'

There's a story that during the Second World War – when a whole nation was praying for deliverance even though humanly speaking all seemed lost – an officer sent a message from the beaches at Dunkirk to British military headquarters. It contained just three words, 'But if not'. Apparently, Churchill recognised the biblical reference. This Christian officer was choosing to stand with Job, with Habakkuk, and with three young men who, when faced with death by fire, had said:

> 'King Nebuchadnezzar ... If we are thrown into the blazing furnace, the God we serve is able to deliver us from it ... *But even if he does not*, we want you to know, Your Majesty, that we will not serve your gods or worship the image of gold you have set up.'
>
> Daniel 3:16–18, (my emphasis)

Don't get me wrong – I'm not looking for trouble. Even just reading the book of Job scares me. And I suppose the truth is that I'd prefer there *was* a deal – to keep my family from harm, my body from illness, my ministry blessed and my critics at bay. But in my heart, I know that real love doesn't operate on the basis of a deal. And when those difficult times come, I pray that by his grace I will know the strength of that anchor in the storm, which will enable me to pray, 'Lord please deliver me from this. But if not ...'

ROB PARSONS, OBE

Rob is the founder and chairman of Care for the Family, and he has spoken across the world to more than a million people on family and parenting issues. He is the bestselling author of nearly 30 books, including *The Sixty Minute* Series and *From The Heart: An honest look at life and faith*. Rob is married to Dianne and they live in Cardiff. They have two children and five grandchildren.

ANCHORED IN WORSHIP

LOU FELLINGHAM

When I think of what it means to be anchored in worship, my mind always goes back to my upbringing. It was in some ways a bit of an unlikely foundation, as neither of my parents had any church background whatsoever. It all started when the pastor of a local church knocked on their door one day and invited them to come along on Sunday. They told him they would go, but they didn't. So this persistent pastor came back the next week and said, 'You didn't come to church, and I was hoping to see you. Perhaps next Sunday – I'd love to see you there.' I recognise this might seem overly pushy to some, and perhaps it was. But it worked. They went along and Mum became a Christian, then shortly after, Dad did the same.

So from then on, my four sisters and I were growing up in a Christian home, and it was a house filled with music – Andraé Crouch, Keith Green, Amy Grant and also a little Stevie Wonder! Sundays were my favourite days. In my teenage years we headed up the road to church in the morning and came back for family lunch, bringing in tow anyone who needed a home to hang out in. Afternoons were usually filled with old musicals (love me a bit of Doris Day!) and then back to church in the evening. We'd have crumpets for supper and then the week would begin again. Every morning before school, my dad would read from a booklet of short devotionals called *Our Daily Bread*, and we would rouse ourselves in the last few minutes to mumble out a prayer – then off we'd pop for the day. We were loved and encouraged in God, and I am truly grateful.

At the age of five, I gave my life to Jesus. When I was seven, I started singing harmony at the front of the church and I loved telling people about Jesus through song. As I got older, I joined choirs, bands, made demo tapes and continued to figure out what it was to love God. I loved to sing hymns with gusto and joy, but it was when I was fifteen that I truly began to recognise the presence and work of the Holy Spirit. This led me to discover how integral the Holy Spirit is to my walk in Christ and how much more there to was to know.

Part of this discovery was moving to Brighton to join a band called Phatfish where I would worship alongside David Fellingham – a songwriter, worship leader and pastor at the time (my father-in-law now) and Stuart Townend. I married the drummer from the band, Nathan, and we now have three amazing children. During these years I have continued to learn about the Holy Spirit and the role of worship in our everyday lives. I can honestly say that these times have been transformative in my walk and growth as a Christian.

Now, in case my early life all sounds a bit too *Little House on the Prairie* to you, let me assure you that although I did have an amazing upbringing, I am in no way perfect, and life hasn't always been that perfect either.

2008 was the year it happened. My mum had been feeling under the weather. She mentioned not feeling right in February. In May she went to the doctor where they discovered a small mass in her womb. In July it had grown at a rapid rate, so the medical team suggested an operation at the end of August to remove the mass and do a biopsy.

When Mum went in for the operation, they discovered the mass had ruptured. They removed as much as they could and hoped for the best. For the next six weeks my mum was in agony – in and out of hospital and becoming a shadow of herself. It was awful.

Towards the end of the six weeks we knew that time was running out. We gathered together as sisters, along with our husbands, and camped out at our parents' house for a week. There are many traumatic details from those few days and not all of them are mine to tell, but needless to say it was a very difficult and painful time. My mum was my hero, and I loved her deeply. I did not want her to go. I knew that sudden healings were possible with God, but as ever, the question of 'will he?' loomed over us. As time wore on, we felt that her days left on earth were numbered. It was beyond hard as I watched my dad never leave her side and my mum pass from this life to the next. Life would never be the same.

She died on Tuesday 14th October 2008. Even as I write this, I feel the tears well up and my heart ache.

A vivid memory for me over those few days before she left was on the Saturday night. All of us gathered around her bedside and worshipped. We sang songs together, read Scripture, prayed and wept. It was probably one of the most tangible moments I have felt the Lord near in my entire life. The words of those Scriptures and songs never had more profound meaning than they did at that moment. The promises of eternal life, of the age to come, of seeing Jesus face-to-face – all of these came into sharp view, and the comfort and peace of the Holy Spirit was so moving. What was happening was not what we wanted at all, but as we worshipped, as we centred ourselves on the truth and the power of the gospel, God met with us in a deep way.

Over the next few weeks, I had to keep surrendering my heart's desire of wanting my mum back to the hope that we have for eternity and trusting God. I knew the truth, but I had to give myself time for my heart and soul to align. Grief should never be washed over or cheapened because of our hope. For me, it was essential throughout this process to anchor myself in worship. Because of my relationship with God, I was already in the place of trust and surrender before this moment. When this whirlwind came and tore through my life, my house was built on the rock and was steady.

I have a few worship-related memories from the time after Mum passed. One was being unable to properly sing. As you might have gathered, I've always been one of those annoying people who sings around the house and turns everything into a song – it's hard to shut me up! For a season after Mum passed, however, my song turned into a groan. I was not able to 'dance before the Lord with joy'. I was not able to make any sort of powerful declaration. All I could do was pour out a groan to the Lord. It was from the pit of my stomach and was the only offering I had.

Soon after Mum's passing, I was in a church service. We were singing, 'You're all I want, You're all I ever needed,' and I couldn't say that was true at the time. I was thinking, 'Actually, I want my mum!' I had to remove myself at that point to have a good cry and chat to the Lord about it. Then there was the time when I was driving and the song on the stereo was 'Hallelujah, our God reigns'. I lost it. I howled as my spirit testified to this truth that no matter how painful this was, no matter how hard, this truth of God reigning was greater, so in my tears I offered my worship to God. Now, don't get me wrong – this is not about erasing grief, or about how 'well' I coped with it – I was devastated. My soul experienced deep sorrow. But it is all about how wonderful God is. As we worship, as we gaze on him, as we trust in his faithfulness and the power of the cross now and for eternity, that's when we find the 'peace that passes all understanding' (Philippians 4:7).

Grief should never be washed over or cheapened because of our hope.

To pour out our anguish in worship is not to say that it's fine that all this terrible stuff happened – far from it! Rather, it is bringing an offering of trust and dependence on God and reminding our souls that we have our hope in Jesus, despite the trials of life. We are made to worship Jesus now, fix our eyes on him now, but currently we only see him in part. Our hope is that one day, he will return and then we will be worshipping him forever, singing 'Holy Holy Holy.' In the coming kingdom of heaven, worship is a state we will forever be in.

It is God's kindness to us that worship exists. He doesn't need it. It doesn't make him greater than he already is. It is a wonderful gift he has given us, one which allows us not only to take our eyes off ourselves but to put them onto a wonderful, incredible, holy God. Worship is not about pretending that everything is OK. When we look at the Psalms, we see they are full of cries about life not being OK, where the reality of life and trauma is seen plainly, but also the heart response of worship is found alongside it.

> 'Why, my soul, are you downcast? Why so disturbed within me? Put your hope in God, for I will yet praise him, my Saviour and my God.'
>
> Psalm 43:5

The very act of turning towards God, rather than away, is an act of worship – even in our pain, grief, or anger. And although this is our choice, the Bible speaks of the Spirit helping us in our weakness (Romans 8:26–27). We don't have to be reliant on our strength or ability – we need only ask the Spirit to help us.

How do we respond?

We all have seasons in life where we are downcast, when our souls don't feel particularly 'well'. We live in a broken world, and because of this, there are innumerable challenges that life throws our way. You might be in a season of grief and loss, facing difficulties in your relationships with others, struggling with burnout or overwhelm, have major health concerns, be navigating unexpected change or be deeply invested in helping others bear their burdens. Whatever you are walking through right now, whether it's a combination of these things or other concerns, we will all experience difficult times. As Christians, we know that our hearts are prone to wander, and we won't always respond to difficulty in the most helpful manner. But I want

If we ask God, he will help us to learn how to live with childlike faith and keep Jesus at the centre of it all.

to encourage you that in worship, not only can we draw close to God, he will draw near to us. When we lift our eyes to him, both figuratively and literally, we can come in joy or pain, strength or weakness, triumph or brokenness. And God in his grace blesses us and speaks to us as we bring our offering.

Consider what Paul says in his letter to the Roman Christians:

> 'So here's what I want you to do, God helping you: Take your everyday, ordinary life – your sleeping, eating, going-to-work, and walking-around life – and place it before God as an offering. Embracing what God does for you is the best thing you can do for him.'
>
> Romans 12:1, MSG

This means that we worship with our whole selves – every part of our being, all surrendered to God and for him.

I remember seeing this in action some years ago at a Christian conference. It was a rarity that I wasn't actually involved in leading, but was looking after my sister's kids. During a time of worship, I turned around and saw two ladies with their arms raised high, with tears streaming down their faces. It so happened that I knew the backstory and circumstances of their lives, and their situations were really difficult at that moment. There was a lot of rubbish happening, but their response was to raise their hands and to offer their worship to God. It struck me so much that I wrote a song about it, called *Sacrifice*. One of the lyrics simply says, 'Surrendering again, broken before You'. My hope was (and is) that this would capture how we all feel at times.

It's a stance that echoes the 'Still I will praise You' moments often written in the Psalms. Now as a songwriter, I do have a soft spot for the Psalms, and chapter 23 is a personal favourite (as it is for many of us!). It's poetic, instantly relatable and helpfully, it's memorable. I find that there is so much even in the first sentence: 'The Lord is my Shepherd; I shall not want'. Sometimes that is enough to rest in. And it's reassuring that when you look at the Psalms, they aren't ecstatically happy all the way through – there are some Psalms that seem to shout, 'Where the heck are you, God? My enemies are after me!'. But often, having said something like this, the Psalmist will say, 'Still I will praise you'. Surrender and brokenness really can walk hand in hand.

I remember a friend of mine who had suffered several miscarriages telling me that when she came to God in her times of worship, she struggled to say anything. She had no words – the pain was so deep. She simply got on her knees and raised her hands before him. She put on the song *Sacrifice*, and cried from her heart the simple refrain 'I worship you'. Life didn't suddenly become perfect, but she told me that in that moment she felt God meeting with her in her sorrow.

Friends, we are all prone to look away from God and get distracted with life. Disappointment can calcify into cynicism, and our seemingly unanswered prayers can feel like they are going to swallow us up. But if we ask God, he will help us to learn how to live with childlike faith and keep Jesus at the centre of it all. The Holy Spirit is available at all times. He never leaves you or forsakes you. Let's spend time with him, so that we know him more.

> 'So don't be afraid, little flock. For it gives your Father great happiness to give you the Kingdom.'
>
> Luke 12:32, NLT

LOU FELLINGHAM

Lou is a songwriter and an internationally known worship leader. She is known for her prophetic edge, distinctive voice, and unwavering energy to see lives changed through the power of music and words. Lou is married to Nathan and they have three children. They live in Brighton where they enjoy being outdoors, sharing food with others, leading worship at Emmanuel Church and hanging with friends and family.

ANCHORED IN PURPOSE

MARK CHESTER

Sometime in my childhood, I decided that I wanted to find and have a relationship with the person who had created me. In fact, given the intimate knowledge my creator would have of me, I felt he would know best how I should live my life, and that if I invited him he would open doors of opportunity and through them I would walk. The path would be distinct, my purpose clear. All would be well. But it did not turn out to be as straightforward as I thought.

My parents believed in God and that belief had influenced their decisions and shaped their lives. During my early years, my father moved careers, my mother took on unpaid community roles, and we left the safe harbour of family and friends in Liverpool to relocate to the north Wales countryside, where they helped to start a new church – all because they were trying to figure out and follow God's will. God was evident to me in their values, habits and behaviours. They thanked him for food before we ate it, consulted him about decisions big and small, read the Bible with my brother and me and worshipped him at church every Sunday. So I began to believe in him too.

It wasn't easy growing up believing in God, trying to please him. I didn't think God would want me to swear or lie, to cheat or gossip or to allow greed or lust to gain a foothold in my heart. But I also wanted to fit in with those around me, melt into the crowd, be anonymous. The fear of ridicule for being different needled away at me. It was uncomfortable, and consequently I was anxious to leave my youth and enter a more adult world as quickly as I could. I didn't waste any time glancing over my shoulder; I was ready to leap into a more mature future. My peers were destined for university. I decided that I was not, and I began to search for what I could do with my life, to find a role in which I could feel useful and fulfilled, to look for a purpose. I found my way to a civil service desk, but within months of picking up my government-issue pen and memo pad, I knew I had not found what God wanted me to do with my life. Surely, there was something else; there had to be.

I always thought that God would waste no time in leading me to my sweet spot of purpose. Perhaps there would be a short period of preparation, but it would be quickly followed by a lifetime of serving him in the role he had set aside specifically for me. But that was not how things would pan out. It seems it often isn't God's way. I spent year after year constrained by the red tape of officialdom, and despite searching hard for something else, no doors opened. Was this my life's lot? I didn't want to appear ungrateful. I knew it was an excellent job – secure, good pay and a first-rate pension – but it just didn't feel like the right thing for me.

One of the hardest things for a child to learn is how to wait. But it's a lesson we must all learn. A modern version of an old book of poetic laments talks about passionately waiting and quietly hoping (Lamentations 3:25–27, MSG). This seems to me to be the key to developing a healthy sense of patience. But that was not a lesson I'd learnt back then. In searching for my purpose I was becoming frustrated, agitated even. And then it happened: my daughter Megan was born, and under the mentorship of a good friend, Dirk Uitterdijk, I felt I had at last found my purpose. I decided I was to be the best father I could be and help others to be good dads too. It would be several more years – and another child, my son Billy – before I was able to translate my purpose into a career in family support work.

How, even in the smallest of acts, can we bring more love into the world?

You may be reading this and thinking how fortunate I was to find a purpose at all. Perhaps you've been seeking your purpose for decades. Maybe you feel unfulfilled, resentful even. You may expect me to encourage you to just keep on passionately waiting and quietly hoping for your life's purpose to be revealed to you. But I have a slightly different perspective now, the benefit of the long view. Diligently seeking what we're meant to be doing with our lives is, I believe, a good thing, but we can become so fixated with the grand plan and with what comes next that we can overlook purpose in the moments of each day. I certainly did. Finding purpose can be within closer reach than we imagine. What is coming our way this day? What responsibilities do we have?

Where will we go? Who will we meet? Who depends upon us? How, even in the smallest of acts, can we bring more love into the world? No time need be wasted in living a purposeful life. Meaning can be found in the nitty-gritty of our daily existence.

I lost my sense of purpose for a while. I had always thought I was pretty emotionally stable, with not too many highs or lows, and felt that I took stressful situations in my stride. I was working at Liverpool Football Club, delivering a programme called Tactics 4 Families in the city's schools, and was going through a particularly testing spell. I'd never been a crier, but one evening at the end of an arduous week I was shocked to find myself weeping uncontrollably, and I couldn't stop. In the coming days and weeks I would shed enough tears to make up for lost time. I was firmly in the throes of a breakdown, and it was a huge shock. I stopped going to work, I stayed in bed and slept a lot. I struggled to find purpose in anything for a while, save for getting out of bed and managing to make it through each day – but perhaps that was enough. The only way I was going to rebuild my emotional self was by simplifying my life and by concentrating my efforts on rediscovering some hope for the future. That struggle – to find meaning, to restore hope – became a purpose in itself. It is what kept me going. And there it is again – that nitty-gritty purpose that comes for us, if we let it, through the fundamentals of living each day. My breakdown changed me – for better as well as for worse – and since then I've had a greater appreciation for the ordinary, everyday experiences and tasks, the brass tacks of survival. There is meaning in the mundane.

When Jesus walked the earth, he was here for a purpose, a huge purpose. He had been sent by his Father to save humankind from the hopelessness of unbelief and wrongdoing. The grandest of callings. Such a vast undertaking, and yet integral was the attention Jesus gave to his everyday encounters, conversations and experiences. Talking with a woman at a well, giving a helping hand at a party, visiting a tax collector, making breakfast for his friends on the beach. Purpose can be found in both the commonplace and the weightier vocation at the same time. They are not mutually exclusive.

In March 2016 a man called Bob Ebeling died in Utah at the age of 89. He was an ordinary man, and yet he was also a remarkable man. 30 years before Bob died, he made a phone call that was full of purpose, but it failed in its objective, and as a result, he lived the following three decades with persistent guilt.

Bob was working as an engineer for a NASA contractor, and the morning before the space shuttle Challenger launched, he called his boss at the Kennedy Space Center to warn him that low overnight temperatures could stiffen the rubber seals and cause rocket fuel to leak – and that would lead to disaster. A meeting was convened. Bob and others presented their concerns, but the powers-that-be decided to ignore their warnings and press on with the launch.

73 seconds into Challenger's flight it exploded, killing the seven crewmembers. Bob Ebeling was watching in a crowded conference room and could do nothing but weep. He would go on to fall into a deep depression, which prompted his retirement, and 30 years later the pain was still lingering. In an interview with NPR two months before he died, Bob said, 'I think that was one of the mistakes that God made. He shouldn't have picked me for that job ... But next time I talk to him, I'm gonna ask him, "Why me? You picked a loser."'[15]

[15] Howard Berkes, 'Your Letters Helped Challenger Shuttle Engineer Shed 30 Years Of Guilt', *NPR*, 25 February 2016 [accessed 15 July 2024]

We can think that once we've discovered purpose, whether that be within a grand calling or in the minutiae of our lives, everything will go swimmingly. Outcomes will take care of themselves. But that wasn't the case for Bob Ebeling, and he lived with debilitating disappointment. Of course, Bob wasn't a loser and God did pick the right man to fulfil his purpose, because Bob did exactly what he should have done. People who listened to that interview with Bob, including some who had been involved in the decision to launch Challenger, wrote and reassured him that he had nothing to feel guilty about, and so his burden was eased a little before he died. Bob's story makes me remember that the validity of our purpose cannot be judged by the quality of the outcome. We must just do the right thing and hope.

Purpose can be found in both the commonplace and the weightier vocation at the same time. They are not mutually exclusive.

I have to confess that once I discovered my 'grand purpose' – to support relationships between dads and their children – I thought I was going to change the world on a momentous scale. I have not. But I have done what I thought God wanted me to do. I have come to accept that I may see a smaller-scale outcome than I had imagined, but this does not make my purpose less valuable. In fact, I believe it is as significant as the callings of those who have been honoured with medals and statues. If we help change one person's life, we've changed the world.

Purpose is about what motivates us, what makes us get out of bed in the morning and live another day. After I had my breakdown, when I struggled to find any purpose whatsoever and was not able to cope with even small amounts of responsibility, I wrote down five questions and asked them of myself each morning soon after waking. They were:

- Who can I pray for?
- Who can I thank?
- What can I give away?
- Who should I send a message to?
- Who should I spend time with?

These questions gave me a purpose to live each day. They took me away from myself, made me think of others, encouraged me to be grateful and enabled me to feel that God was using me to do good, despite my limited capabilities.

In the film *Chariots of Fire*, the runner Eric Liddell is portrayed as saying, 'I believe that God made me for a purpose. For China. But he also made me fast. And when I run I feel his pleasure. To give it up would be to hold him in contempt.'[16]

If you are struggling to find what you feel is a worthy purpose for today, maybe a good place to start is to ask yourself what God has given you, how he has made you and where he has placed you. The things we do with our days may seem simple and inconsequential. Books may not be written about our lives, films may not be made – but God has always had an eye for the unassuming and unremarked.

So think of this: when do you feel God's pleasure most? Because perhaps that is where, today, you will find purpose.

[16] *Chariots of Fire*, dir. Hugh Hudson, 1981.

MARK CHESTER

Mark is the men's support manager at Care for the Family and a popular event speaker. He is the founder of *Who Let The Dads Out?* – a movement of churches reaching out to fathers and their children. He is the author of two books including *The Soul of Football: One man's story of football, family and faith*. Mark is married to Su and they live in Cheshire. They have two children.

ANCHORED IN PRAYER

PAULA PRIDHAM

'Prayer should be the key of the day and the lock of the night.'

Anonymous

On the third day of my battle with Covid, I woke late, mindful to avoid my husband Tom so that he wouldn't get infected. I called out to ask him to make me porridge for breakfast. He responded with a grunt and shuffled downstairs. Minutes later, he returned. I went to say thank you and found him sitting on the spare room bed. He muttered, 'I think I've had a stroke.'

With a four-hour wait for an ambulance and hospitals not admitting anyone with Covid, I urgently called a neighbour to take him to the local A&E. Tom could walk, but his speech was slurred, and time was critical.

Thus began the most harrowing 24 hours of my life.

At 4:15pm, a garbled text from Tom arrived: 'Hi sweetheart. I may for some time. Sorry to let do.' My response garnered no reply. Later, a doctor informed me that emergency stroke treatment caused a brain bleed, leaving Tom's left side paralysed. He was unable to eat or drink, and was barely conscious. They were monitoring him, uncertain of the next steps.

Denying the severity, I focused on practicalities – work, Tom's pastoral duties in church and my upcoming residential course. I asked others to pray, sought God's intervention, and declined offers of company. By 8.00pm, after handling logistics, I broke down, begging and bargaining with God for Tom's recovery, venting anger and sorrow.

God brought me solace through Psalm 30:5: 'Weeping may stay for the night, but rejoicing comes in the morning.'

At 11.00pm, despite my plea for solitude, friends arrived, followed by an update from the doctor. Tom's condition had worsened, and the outlook was grim. He would possibly need brain surgery. My friends organised prayer and stayed with me through the night. By dawn, Tom had stabilised. Surgery was averted, and he was moved to a stroke unit. My friends departed, leaving me alone with the verse that sustained me.

Tom spent three months in hospital, relearning to walk but with enduring limitations. Yet the ordeal brought us closer to each other and to God. Reflecting on this, I realise how my prayer life had faltered up until that point, surviving solely by God's grace. This trial taught me much, particularly about prayer.

Being rooted in prayer anchors us in God's steadfast love and presence. It's the lifeline equipping us to face each day with courage and assurance. If you're already a prayer warrior, cherish that gift – we need you. If, like me, you've struggled in prayer, felt inadequate, or doubted if God heard you, let me share what I've learnt.

What is prayer, really?

Grammatically, prayer serves many functions:

- As a verb – 'to pray'
- As a noun – 'We said a prayer' or 'We spent time in prayer'
- As a ceremony – 'Silent prayer honoured the person'
- As a religious service – 'Evening prayers'

Yet these definitions don't capture its essence. Prayer is our direct line to God, facilitating two-way communication with our Creator. It's how we express gratitude, seek help, confess wrongs, and find wisdom, guidance, comfort and strength through his Word.

Prayer is conversing with our loving God, who desires our communication. Whether our prayers are eloquent or muddled, long or brief, formal or messy, God values their sincerity.

Honest prayer doesn't require pretence, as God understands our hearts.

1 Thessalonians 5:16–18 urges us to pray continually, rejoicing and giving thanks in all circumstances, as this is God's will for us in Christ Jesus.

In Tom's stroke crisis, I prayed ceaselessly, though not with gratitude. Yet I had much to be thankful for: Christian friends who acted swiftly, ignoring my prideful independence, and a resilient NHS service, flawed yet invaluable.

I don't believe God held my anger or lack of thankfulness against me in the midst of anguish. That's all part of the messiness of honest prayer. Honest prayer doesn't require pretence, as God understands our hearts.

Establishing a prayerful life

> 'True prayer is a way of life, not just for emergencies. Make it a habit, and in need, you'll be prepared.'[17]

Jesus exemplifies a rich prayer life. He would have engaged in formal group prayers at the synagogue, but we know he also sought solitude or met with a few disciples to pray. He taught his followers, using what we call the Lord's Prayer. This prayer was an intimate experience with their Father – Abba – and Jesus emphasised that it need not be lengthy. The Lord's Prayer is just 66 words long.

Jesus prayed at pivotal moments, in diverse places and for different purposes. I've found his spontaneous prayers liberating. Now, in a stalled discussion at work or with friends, I freely seek clarity with a swift prayer. If I'm trying to make a decision, I stop and ask for wisdom. Prayer was integral to Jesus' life. He didn't so much have a prayer life, rather a life of prayer.

One key lesson I've learned is not to compare myself to others. My first prayer meeting as a new Christian was daunting. Assigned a topic, I awaited my turn with mounting anxiety as each person in the semicircle spoke out their prayer. I felt pressured to speak, unsure what to say. When my turn came, words tumbled out incoherently. To this day I can't remember what I said. The experience left me with the feeling of inadequacy for years. It has taken a while for me to

---

[17] Billy Graham, '10 Quotes from Billy Graham on Prayer', *The Billy Graham Library*, 5 March 2019 [accessed 17 July 2024].

become less self-absorbed and self-critical, and to realise that God really is just pleased to hear from me at all! Not all of us are able to have a beautiful turn of phrase, but when we hear one we should allow ourselves to be blessed by it, rather than condemned.

I also have the kind of mind that finds it easy to wander. Who knew that once I set myself up for a time of prayer, I'd get a sudden desire to hoover? I don't have this urge at any other time! But I believe this experience of distraction is common to many of us. The enemy of our souls really doesn't want us to pray and so we shouldn't be surprised when distractions come along. The key is to recognise them for what they are and set them to one side. No need to beat ourselves up or feel unworthy – just pray.

Concern about finding the perfect words can stall our prayers. Using Scripture eases this fear. The Psalms offer rich expressions. Pray Psalm 119:33–40 for guidance or Psalm 63:1–8 for closeness to God. Insert your name, or the name of someone you are praying for, into the Psalm. For example Psalm 46:1–3 and verse 11 would become:

> 'God is my/Tom's refuge and strength, an ever-present help in trouble.
>
> Therefore I/he will not fear though the earth give way, and the mountains fall into the heart of the sea,
>
> though its waters roar and foam and the mountains quake with their surging
>
> ...
>
> The Lord Almighty is with me/Tom; The God of Jacob is my/his fortress.'

There is also a beauty in formal written prayers, some of which have been used by Christians before us for hundreds of years. Although not an Anglican, I have found great comfort and meaning in using *The Book of Common Prayer* during a service – as much as I have in extempore prayer.

If you are new to prayer or struggling in your prayer life, start with just one small step. If you're an introvert, you might find it works best for you to find a special, quiet place. This might be a prayer corner in the home, a garden seat under a tree or a solo prayer walk. On the other hand, if you prefer the energy of being around others, commit to a prayer group, buddy up with a prayer partner, or go prayer walking with someone. As you pass each house, pray for those who live there.

If we keep at these little things, we'll soon find that we have built a beautiful habit, whether that's saying a short prayer to start and finish the day, grace before we eat, or praying through the Psalms during a lunch break.

It's not just about us

God wants us to pray for others and ourselves, but prayer shouldn't just be a list of requests. It's praise, gratitude, stillness and hearing God's voice. These deepen our relationship with him. Praising God transcends daily life, prompting awe and thankfulness. As we focus on God, it leads us to a place of thankfulness and repentance and allows God to speak to us – maybe not audibly, but through an inner sense or hearing his voice.

Initially, this felt odd. Silence discomforted me, and discerning God's voice among my own thoughts was challenging. Unsure, I tested thoughts against Scripture, discussing with trusted friends. When I focused on God, not myself, I experienced intimacy and closeness with him.

Once, during an aid trip to Romania in the late 80s, my team and I faced a challenge at the Hungarian-Romanian border. We were supposed to be met by a pastor from Romania, but due to delays he was not there when we arrived late at night. In an unfamiliar town with six people relying on me, I turned to prayer, deciding not to move until I felt guided by God. Before long, I felt directed to a specific street where I would find a hotel. Initially doubting the thought, its persistence convinced me to act on it.

Following the directions, we indeed found a hotel. We sat in the reception area, having a drink and figuring out our next steps. Just then, the Romanian pastor arrived. He had been delayed as well and, lacking a passport, prayed at the border. Remarkably, the guards let him through, and he too was directed by God to the same hotel.

I would love to say that has been a common occurrence in my life, but it has been the exception. Mostly, I live by trusting that my prayers are heard.

When prayers seem unanswered

> 'Even if all the things that people prayed for happened – which they do not – this would not prove what Christians mean by the efficacy of prayer. For prayer is request. The essence of request, as distinct from compulsion, is that it may or may not be granted. And if an infinitely wise Being listens to the requests of finite and foolish creatures, of course He will sometimes grant and sometimes refuse them.'[18]

There have been more times in my life when God appears to be in silent mode rather than full volume. Going back

[18] C. S. Lewis, 'The Efficacy of Prayer' in *The World's Last Night and Other Essays* (HarperCollins, 2017), p.59.

to the time of Tom's stroke, while God blessed me with the verse that carried me through the night, my prayers for Tom to be fully healed have not been answered. Perhaps more accurately, they have not been answered with an unequivocal yes. I have come to believe, however, that God always answers, but not always with the answer we are looking for. It could be: 'Yes', 'No', 'Not yet', or even 'You do it'.

Prayer is a lifelong journey. It's not about perfection but about growing closer to God each day.

This is when prayer becomes a mystery. I have no idea why prayers are sometimes not answered to the satisfaction of the person praying. I have no doubt that God hears; I have no doubt God can and does act. I have no doubt that God is good, knows all things, and only wants the best. So I hang on to Jesus' words in the Garden of Gethsemane, 'Yet not my will, but yours' (Luke 22:42).

Am I disappointed when the answer to my prayer seems to be 'No' or 'Not yet', or it feels like my prayer is unanswered? Absolutely, because of course I know best! Then I come down to earth and remember that I don't. There may be many reasons we do not get a 'Yes' to our requests, and the danger is that we may think that God does not love us or that we're not good enough. None of which are true. What is true is that God knows why 'Yes' isn't the best answer, and that is something I have had to accept in faith.

Being anchored

Remember, prayer is a lifelong journey. It's not about perfection but about growing closer to God each day. Throughout my ordeal with Tom's stroke and the subsequent months of recovery, prayer emerged as a steadfast anchor, guiding me through the darkest moments and reminding me of God's unwavering presence.

This experience taught me the value of honest, heartfelt prayer and the importance of cultivating a prayerful life. It revealed that God cherishes our genuine communication, whether eloquent or messy, and that prayer is not just about seeking answers but also about finding solace, strength and a deeper connection with our Creator.

Building a habit of prayer involves embracing its many forms, from spontaneous utterances to structured liturgies, and recognising that distractions and doubts are natural. It's about trusting that God hears us, even in silence, and that his responses – whether 'Yes', 'No', 'Not yet', or 'Do it yourself' – are rooted in his profound love and wisdom.

In the end, prayer is more than a ritual; it's a lifeline that sustains us, transforms us, and brings us closer to God.

PAULA PRIDHAM

Paula is a director at Care for the Family, where she has worked for 25 years. She has a PGDip in Spiritual Formation and is part of the leadership team of a small – in number, but big in heart – chapel in South Wales. Paula is married to Tom and they live in Cardiff.

ANCHORED IN HOPE

STEVE LEGG

In April 2023, my wife Bekah and I sat in a hospital waiting room. These places are depressing at the best of times. The walls are littered with posters about cancer, and the leaflets and booklets are terrible too. They explain how cancers can appear in the weirdest places – and I don't mean Littlehampton. There's adenoid, appendix and penile cancer, to name just three of the more unusual ones. It would be like sitting in a hairdresser's with pictures of hairstyles gone badly wrong. Why not have a TV on? *Homes Under The Hammer* or even *Casualty* would be better than staring blankly at a wall.

We were waiting to hear the results of scans that we hoped would show that the melanoma which had steadily crept into my body over the last year had been halted in its tracks. We hoped that the scans would show a body clear of tumours. We hoped that all would be well.

But as the doctor came to call us in, her face told a different story, and hope began to wither. The following 20 minutes replaced that hope with a stone-cold feeling of dread. The oncologist kindly but clearly explained that the cancer had spread to my liver, spine, and brain and that it was present throughout my abdomen. She explained that there were only palliative treatments left to try and that the natural progression of the disease gave me around five months to live.

It felt as if the hope was literally sucked from my body in those moments as I came to terms with my mortality, with the lack of control I had over not just my own future, but my family's future. I thought of the hopes and dreams I had for growing old with my wife and watching my five beautiful girls flourish into adulthood.

Life is so often two things at once. Joy is often accompanied by pain.

I had been battling this cancer for 18 months, always believing I would win, and now I was confronted with the reality that you cannot will yourself into wellness, that hoping all will be well does not make it so. Even as we talked about the hopes we had for that summer – to see my first grandchild born, to have a family holiday or to attend my favourite events, I knew that nothing was a guarantee and that these hopes were more dreams that could be snatched away just as quickly as my hope to grow old and grey with Bekah.

Those first days, wrestling with the news, were dark ones. Tears came quickly and often. I was overwhelmed by the sheer volume of love and support from friends and family. My friend Steve arrived with a bag of beers, a family-sized pork pie and lots of love. Others came with hugs, cards and homemade lasagnes. It was beautiful, but it also reminded me of all I would leave behind. Hope was nowhere to be found. Truthfully, hope felt like a fickle friend who could disappear at any moment, leaving disappointment and devastation in its wake instead of a forwarding address.

However, as that first week rolled on, Bekah and I started discussing what we wanted the summer to look like. The doctor had said something, apart from the prognosis, that stuck with us. She had told us that I had a choice – I could live dying, or I could die living. We decided that the second was a far more attractive option. I'd much rather go out with a bang – and no, not from a DIY disaster involving plug sockets (trust me, I've had enough of those) – but in a blaze of glory and a cloud of confetti. So I decided to enjoy all I have and live life to its fullest with every ounce of energy. I figured, why wait for the grand finale when you can have a blast every day?

It was possible because we began to realise that life is so often two things at once. Joy is often accompanied by pain. We had been given the most terrible news, but it had allowed us to make the most of the time I have left. It had brought our family together in a way we wouldn't have experienced otherwise, and it had focused our minds on what and who mattered most. We determined to have a 'summer of joy'. We still had to do all the horrible things that needed doing – wills, conversations about end-of-life care at the hospice and funeral plans. Those things did not bring us joy; they often ended in evenings of tears and holding each other tight. But they didn't need to be all of our world. We could also eat out, walk on the beach, laugh, hold a newborn baby, go to a show and celebrate each day God gave us.

We splashed out and got tickets for *Mamma Mia! The Party* at the O2 Arena in London. It was something we could never usually afford to do. It was like being in a Mediterranean island paradise, sitting at rustic tables in a courtyard with a fountain, olive trees and bougainvillea. We enjoyed a delicious Greek meal as the story and music unfolded around us. It ended with the main floor being transformed into a 1970s disco, where everyone danced to ABBA hits. I say 'everyone danced', but it was my five girls who did that. I watched through tearstained eyes, not because they were terrible dancers but in sheer joy as my very own Dancing Queens let their hair down and danced the night away.

We'd rediscovered hope. Maybe we'd discovered what it really is for the first time. It's more than hoping things go right in our lives, that our football team does well, that we get a promotion at work, or that we'll be returned to total health and see our grandchild born. Hope has to be more than that, and it is – in a world where we can accept that life is two things at once.

Hope, real hope, is so much more and it's inextricably entwined with faith. Faith in what we do not see but in what we know to be true. I could not will myself better; I couldn't even will myself happy, but I could choose to remember what I know to be true. I could choose to remember that I have been created by a God who loves me more than I know, that his plans for my life were written before I was born and that they extend far beyond my time on this earth. I could choose to remember that my wife, my daughters and my unborn grandchild are in his hands, and I can trust him with them. I could choose to remember that even when I can't see it, God is still good. His kingdom is unshakable, which means that as a citizen of heaven, so am I.

There are times when we can't see through the mist of the story that is unfolding around us, but it doesn't mean the sun isn't shining above. We can't always see the bigger picture, but it doesn't mean it's not true. When Jesus was arrested, taken away to a trumped-up trial, beaten and then killed, his followers were left devastated. All their hopes seemed dashed, left in ruins at the foot of the cross where the one they thought would change the world was brutally taken from them. We so swiftly move from Friday to the victory of Sunday that we sometimes miss the in-between. We don't sit with those men and women in the darkness of lost hope; we miss the lessons to be learned in the reality of two things being true simultaneously.

The knowledge of the risen Jesus gives us hope that, in time, the fog will clear and reveal that the sun is still shining. Hope that even in a world that is so uncertain, God is faithful and unchanging.

Even on that first Easter Sunday as three women travelled to the tomb to anoint Jesus' body, they were lost in grief, not even thinking straight as they suddenly realised they didn't have a plan for moving the stone to get access. When they got there and found it already rolled away, they weren't reignited in joy and hope; they were simply afraid. Even when an actual angel told them that Jesus is risen, they didn't celebrate the good news – they couldn't take it in. It was all too overwhelming, and they were left trembling and bewildered.

The big picture was that Jesus was alive, the world had changed, history was turning on its axis, and nothing would be the same again. Good had overcome evil, and death was defeated. But in the smaller picture of the lives of the Marys and Salome, it was also real that they'd watched the one they loved most be beaten and killed. They couldn't find his body, and they didn't understand. Jesus was alive, but they were in despair. Jesus had risen but their hearts were heavy. Hope was right in front of them, but they couldn't see it. Not in that moment. Not yet.

It would take time for the bigger reality to sink in, for it to translate into joy, peace and security. It would take time for that bigger picture to become the hope to which they would anchor their souls and their lives. But in time, that knowledge of the risen Jesus would become the hope that enabled them to face anything.

The fact that this story has been recorded in the Bible gives us hope. Hope that, in time, the fog will clear and reveal that the sun is still shining. Hope that even in a world that is so uncertain, God is faithful and unchanging. Hope that even if my life on earth ends sooner than I'd like, my life in Jesus is eternal. Hope that the story isn't over; it's only just beginning.

That hope has kept me going. It has helped me to wipe away the tears and face the future. It's kept me laughing and seeing the funny side of life. They say laughter is the best medicine (unless you're diabetic … then it's insulin!) And it's true. Hope held me tight when my body betrayed me, pain became my companion, and I grew physically weak. That hope strengthened as my body turned a corner, and for six months I was cancer-free, defying the doctor's predictions. And that hope continues to secure me as more than a year after that initial prognosis, I recover from another surgery and await more results. I do not know what tomorrow holds, but it is well with my soul.

STEVE LEGG

In September 2024, Steve went to be with the Lord.

He was a British speaker, comedian, author and founder of The Breakout Trust. His lifelong passion was for creative communication of the Christian faith. He performed at top venues globally, including Wembley Arena and London's Royal Albert Hall, along with numerous radio and TV appearances. Steve wrote 19 books and founded the men's Christian lifestyle magazine *Sorted*, which had 80,000 readers in 26 countries. Steve lived with his wife Bekah in Littlehampton, and together they had five daughters.

ANCHORED IN PEACE

PAUL FRANCIS

For most of my life I have battled with my emotional and mental wellbeing, and the search for peace is, at times, a struggle. Sometimes on my journey I feel at peace, yet at other times it seems far away.

Maybe I'm showing my age by saying this, but one of my favourite songs is U2's *I Still Haven't Found What I'm Looking For*. Over the years of my journey with Jesus, I have found the lyrics very relatable. U2's lead singer Bono, a follower of Jesus, who has always been upfront about his faith, nevertheless confesses in this song that there is an ineffable *something* that he's been looking for, which he has not yet found.

Despite his faith in Jesus, Bono still has a yearning in his inner being. He is still searching for peace.

Bono is far from alone in his sentiments (as the enduring popularity of this song would seem to attest!). For many years I thought this song was about people of no faith who are searching for meaning, and I still believe that it is relatable to people of all faiths and none. However, more recently, I have realised it is true of me – and indeed, of many more of us who follow Jesus than we might care to admit. Although I follow Jesus, something inside of me says: 'But I still haven't found what I'm looking for'.

We need to practice silence and solitude for the sake of our souls and wellbeing – it is the door into peace.

In talking to and observing people over the years, especially in my capacity as a church leader, I've discovered that a lack of fulfilment in life and of peace is a common experience that many people share. Deep within us, there is a constant yearning for more. We are pilgrims on a journey with God, and until we see him face to face there will always be a longing for more.

I'm a visual learner and so I love images. One that has helped me greatly is described in my favourite Psalm:

> 'My heart is not proud, LORD,
> my eyes are not haughty;
> I do not concern myself with great matters
> or things too wonderful for me.
> But I have calmed and quieted myself,
> I am like a weaned child with its mother;
> like a weaned child I am content.'

Psalm 131:1–2

I love this image – a beautiful picture of a child, secure and satisfied in her mother's arms, in utter peace and contentment. The place where I want to be.

So where does my journey with peace begin?

It starts with knowing that God loves me.

It starts with contenting myself in the Father's love.

It starts with resting in Jesus, the source of our peace.

Knowing that God loves me

> 'I have calmed and quieted myself'
>
> Psalm 131:2

Bono sings of the cross in his famous song, describing how Jesus broke the bonds of sin and shame that bind us. For those of us who have found faith, whether it happened almost in an instant or over months or years, at some point we experienced the truth of these words. We became followers of Jesus. He healed our brokenness. He loosed our chains. He carried our cross of shame. And we embraced it!

But sometimes, it's hard to let ourselves *feel* it.

This is what the psalmist is addressing above, and it is interesting where he starts: 'My heart is not proud … my eyes are not haughty'. Truly knowing God's love requires us to lay down our self-reliance and any arrogance we may have unconsciously absorbed. In order to rest in his love, we have to want God more than anything else, as another Psalm describes: 'You, God, are my God, earnestly I seek you; I thirst for you, my whole being longs for you' (Psalm 63:1).

We live in a world that conspires to keep us busy and distracted. When we get bored, we look at social media, check messages, watch a video, or stream a Spotify playlist. We get in the car and put the radio on. In fact, we have an unlimited ability to fill our time with near-constant noise. Our lifestyle does not encourage us to stop and simply be. It sometimes seems that everything in life works against us 'stopping', especially in order to seek and know more of God.

As author Andrew Sullivan has commented:

> 'There are books to read; landscapes to be walked; friends to be with; life to be fully lived … This new epidemic of distraction is our civilization's specific weakness. And its threat is not so much to our minds, even as they shape-shift under pressure. The threat is to our souls. At this rate, if noise does not relent, we might even forget we have any.'[19]

For most people, the context of silence and solitude is quite daunting. And perhaps the thought of you and God being alone together in silence is daunting too. But as Andrew Sullivan says, we need to practice silence and solitude for the sake of our souls and wellbeing – it is the door into peace.

Contenting myself in the Father's love

> 'Like a weaned child I am content'
>
> Psalm 131:2

Many commentators on this passage have recently pointed out what was not always so obvious to me – a weaned child is a child who is no longer physically dependent on his mother. It is describing a toddler or older, returning to his mother's arms for a cuddle, because he wants to be with her – not, as I had often supposed, a little baby who cannot be anywhere else for sustenance but in his mother's arms. This denotes something important about relationship with God – that at least to some extent, we have the choice of whether or not to content ourselves in his love.

[19] Andrew Sullivan, 'I Used to be a Human Being', *New York Magazine*, 19 September 2016.

Many years ago, I went on retreat to the Northumbria Community, a wonderful place located in beautiful Northumberland. Coming from diverse backgrounds and streams of faith, the community practices a shared life based on the rhythms of Celtic Christianity. As I walked into their large house, I had a real sense of coming home. I knew that the Celtic way was, spiritually, where I felt most at home. St Bede, St Patrick, St David, St Aidan, St Cuthbert and many others – for 27 years they have informed me and shaped who I am. Their spiritual practices have become my own rhythm, one that feeds and sustains me.

When we sit alone in Jesus' presence, we can re-focus our attention on him and allow the Holy Spirit to slowly change us to become more like him.

Of course, not everyone is like me! We are all different, and one of the most important things we can do in our journey towards peace is to discover where we feel at home spiritually. How, for us, we can best follow Jesus and rest in him.

It was while I was at the Northumbria Community that I heard the story of the abbot, the monk and the cell. A young monk went to his abbot to ask for advice about a problem he had. The abbot thought for a while and then said this: 'Go to your cell and the cell will teach you everything.'

The cell, in the monastery, was the room in which the monk slept. It had a single bed, a table, a chair and a cross on the wall. In telling the monk to go there, the abbot was advising him to go to that place where he can be alone with God, spend time with him, and listen to his whispers.

Most of us don't live in a monastery, but the principle behind the abbot's advice is critical for us all. As Pete Greig says: 'I have never found a spiritual shortcut. But I have found that spiritual disciplines, or practices, are a significant part of my journey in learning to walk in peace with God.'[20]

Resting in Jesus, the source of our peace

> 'Peace I leave with you; my peace I give you. I do not give to you as the world gives. Do not let your hearts be troubled and do not be afraid.'
>
> John 14:27

It is both simple and profound: the source of our peace is Jesus – the incomparable Jesus.

In Mark we read that Jesus was up early, taught in the synagogue, healed Peter's mother-in-law during lunch, and late into the evening spent time healing the sick and demonised. At the end of that day, he must have been exhausted. Then Mark writes about the following day: 'Very early in the morning, while it was still dark, Jesus got up, left the house and went off to a solitary place, where he prayed' (Mark 1:35).

Luke records nine times when Jesus went by himself to a quiet place, and elsewhere says that Jesus often withdrew to lonely places and prayed. The way that Jesus sought peace was to set aside time to spend with his Father.

There are many spiritual practices that help us in our walk with God – prayer, reflection, self-examination, creative arts, Sabbath rest, Bible study, discernment, lectio divina, fasting, and works of compassion, to name just a few. All these help us in our walk with God. However, the practices of solitude and silence in particular are ones that are, I think, much needed in these times.

[20] Pete Greig, Lectio 365, 17 October 2023.

Solitude is an appointed place and a time when we stop everything to simply be with God – just him and us. For Jesus, it was somewhere isolated and quiet. The Greek word for this is *eremos,* which also translates as 'desert', 'deserted place', 'desolate place', or 'quiet place'. Jesus went there for 40 days of solitude and silence to prepare himself for what was about to begin.

We may have similar places to go, either regularly or occasionally, but our *eremos* could be a chair that we sit in, a room, a walk, or the car on the drive to work. It could be a snatched five minutes when the baby is quiet! But it's a place where we intentionally stop to focus on God.

In Pete Greig's excellent book on prayer, he tells the story of a conversation he had with Franciscan priest Brennan Manning during the early days of 24/7 Prayer:

> 'Suddenly [Brennan] reached across the table and patted my chest. 'You wanna know how God changes you in here, Pete? Silence! Contemplation! That's how you pray continually.'
>
> 'I hear you,' I said slowly, ... 'But if we all just sit around listening to the silence, how will anything ever get done?'
>
> 'I'm not against intercession and all those other kinds of prayer,' [Brennan] said. 'In fact, I think they're essential. It's just that they are not enough ... '
>
> 'And you think the way to address the world's problems is silence?' I countered.
>
> 'No. I think the way to address the world's problems is *presence*.'' [21]

It's a powerful insight.

---

[21] Pete Greig, *How to Pray: A Simple Guide for Normal People*, pp.122-123.

Solitude and silence also give us the opportunity to take a good look at ourselves and explore who we are. This is captured by Pádraig Ó Tuama, the poet and theologian who wrote this short poem at the age of 15:

> 'And who are you
> When you are alone
> In the dark
> When you are at home?' [22]

Silence and solitude are an opportunity for us to engage with who we are. Things that we have kept hidden in our heart – pain, failure, shortcomings, disappointments, regrets and shame. These things rob us of our peace.

But in the security of God and his love we can bring the 'hidden' into his presence, and not only discover forgiveness and peace through Jesus, but also peace in who we are.

When we sit alone in Jesus' presence, we can re-focus our attention on him and allow the Holy Spirit to slowly change us to become more like him. It is a journey that continues all our lives and we will say, 'I still haven't found what I'm looking for' until we see Jesus face to face.

'And the peace of God, which transcends all understanding, will guard your hearts and your minds in Christ Jesus.'

Philippians 4:7

---

[22] Pádraig Ó Tuama, *In the Shelter: Finding a Home in the World*, (Hodder & Stoughton, 2016) p.136.

PAUL FRANCIS

Paul is the founder of the national charity Going Public, as well as an author and church leader. He has been in Christian ministry for over 30 years and loves reading, good films and TV, creative arts and sport – particularly rugby! He is married to Jane and they live in Cardiff.

PERMISSIONS

Sections of Katharine Hill's chapter 'Anchored in Freedom' first appeared in *Born Free: A Call to be Still, Know God and Flourish in a Hectic World* by Katharine Hill (2023). Reprinted with permission of Muddy Pearl.

Sections of Rob Parsons' chapter 'Anchored in the Veil' first appeared in *From the Heart: An honest look at life and faith* by Rob Parsons (2021). Reprinted with permission of Hodder & Stoughton Ltd.

Permission to print a section of the lyrics to *Cornerstone* by Eric Liljero, Reuben Morgan, Edward Mote, and Jonas Myrin has been granted by Hillsong Australia for the first 5,000 copies of this book.

ACKNOWLEDGMENTS

Many thanks to Jess Hills, Sarah Rowlands, Beth Stevenson, Stephen Hayes, Margaux Doey and John Lambert for their hard work in producing this book.